PATIENCE CARTER

Survive Then Live

The Patience Carter Story

SURVIVE
THEN
LIVE

Contents

1

Pulse

I was sitting in the chair next to Angela, I peeked down at her phone to check the time — it was 1:58 am. Pulse nightclub was about to close soon. My heart didn't want it to, but my body did. My feet were aching and my armpits were drenched. My sleek ponytail had turned into a bushy mess. We embodied the phrase, "leave everything on the dance floor."

Tanya was standing across from us looking down at her phone. Even though we were sitting, she was much shorter than us. We always poked fun at her height. But I didn't have any energy left to crack a joke tonight. So I just giggled to myself and asked her, "How are we getting home?" She swiped across her screen and then said, "We're getting an Uber." That didn't surprise me at all. Angela's parents were 35 minutes away. There was no chance of them coming back to get us. All we had to do was wait. In a few minutes, we were soon going to be heading home and reminiscing about the night we wished had never ended.

But just a few seconds later, a terrifying sound ripped through the air like thunder. In panic, I dropped to the floor. My heart stopped. I felt the noise as much as I heard it. It disrupted my entire spirit. People started screaming in a roar. Bodies were ducking and scrambling for cover.

I had no idea that the sound I heard was from a semi-automatic rifle firing over the music. I didn't see where all the commotion was coming from. I just saw people freezing in shock.

The room warped into one of those escape rooms people lock themselves into for fun. But this one had real danger, and our lives depended on us getting out. Things started moving quickly, it was like the entire room was spinning. I could hear people, but I couldn't hear myself. I was immersed in frenzy. I kept moving backwards away from the chaos. Tanya ran and squatted by the bar, while Angela frantically pivoted back and forth between us until she saw me scooting on the floor — out the exit.

I didn't realize the exit was a few feet away from me. It was like an Angel guided me out the door. I just started crawling backwards faster and faster, then all of a sudden, I felt the cool ground underneath my palms. That's when Angela started coming in my direction and before I knew it she was standing over me and I could see the night sky behind her long curly hair. The wind was still, and the air was slightly crisp. For a moment the sounds were muffled and the short bittersweet reality became clear — we had made it out.

Unfortunately, we all didn't make it out.

I looked up at Angela wide eyed and asked: "Where's Tanya?"

"She's still inside," Angela replied with eyes wider than mine.

"We got to go get her," I said pressing my hands into the ground to lift myself up. Angela nodded her head and like a hero from a movie script, she rushed back inside. There was no hesitation. We didn't know if we were going to get a second chance to escape. But leaving her behind wasn't an option.

The gunfire was still blasting, and it sounded like it was getting closer. In a blur, we saw Tanya squatting by the bar and came to her. She was paralyzed with fear and her eyes looked lost. We didn't have any time to think. The exit seemed too far, and the gunfire sounded way too close. No one ran towards the exit, everyone rushed into the bathrooms. We needed to hide, so we followed them.

We were the last few to enter the bathroom stall we were in. I still didn't understand what was happening. From inside we could hear what sounded like gunshots, and screams. Then suddenly, the music faded out, and all I heard was the repetitive sound of loud gunfire.

Suddenly there was a brief moment of silence. Many of us were chattering trying to make sense of it all. Some people were on their phones, some bleeding, and others were shushing people to remain quiet.

I couldn't process it all at once. I saw a girl bleeding on the floor holding her arm near me, but even then, I couldn't convince my brain that I was about to die. My brain wanted me to believe that I was hearing the sound of a BB gun, not the machine gun the shooter had.

My brain wanted me to SnapChat the moment so my followers could see how far this "Pulse nightclub" would go just to get people out of their club at closing time. But when that brief moment of silence ended, that's when I had to face a horrifying reality — fast. Lightning struck again, this time it was inside our bathroom...

2

No Crystal Stair

I'm no stranger to pain. Each tear I've shed has fueled my indomitable spirit. Each moment of loneliness I've suffered has intensified my faith. And with each hurdle I've surpassed, I have expanded my flexibility. Flexibility to bend greatly under pressure, but remain unbroken.

Every story has a beginning that makes the ending clearer. My beginning was full of challenges. It seemed like I was destined for a life full of sadness. But, little did I know, every heartache I experienced was for my benefit. All of those difficult times growing up prepared me for the worst test of my faith ever.

It was the beginning of summer 2016. I was a fearless 20 year old with an old soul. Things weren't perfect in my life, but I was content. I just finished my second year of college as a first-generation student. I went to New York University, my dream school. My mentor and former NYU Pre-College Professor, Ms. Carolyn, helped me get accepted by writing two recommendation letters to admissions. But I had to work ten times harder to stay. I went from being the smartest girl in the classroom to needing a tutor. And my sophomore year was the toughest. However, I felt more invincible each time I pushed through. That's how I felt that summer— invincible.

I packed up my dorm and headed back to Philadelphia. I didn't want to leave New York, but I had too. I called Philadelphia home, although it never felt like it. I never really had a home. I've always lived with people who weren't my parents. My parents split up when I was two years old. Their marriage was short, really short. It didn't take them long to realize that they brought the worst out in each other. After they separated, my siblings and I lost all contact with our mother. She completely disappeared. We never received any phone call, or visit from our mother since 1998. I tried searching for her on the internet. Unfortunately, after numerous Facebook and Google search sessions, I gave up. I didn't know how to find her. And nobody else went looking for her. Over time, her absence became normal. My siblings had to live with their biological father, and I had to live with my father's mother, Grandma Harriet.

After my Grandma Harriet died, I stayed with a few different family members. I kept shuffling from one toxic situation to another. I eventually landed at my Uncle Derk's house when I was 16 years old. He was one of my dad's brothers. I loved living there at first. He had the nicest house in the family. My uncle wasn't rich, but he was doing well for himself. Everyone loved visiting my uncle's house. He lived in a two story home on a quiet block in Germantown. His wife had impeccable taste, she loved to home decorate. The glamorous chandelier hanging in the dining room could be seen from the front door. Its sparkles greeted guests as they walked inside. There was a gigantic TV, home theater speakers, and recliner sofas in the living room that made every movie worth watching. His refrigerator was always full of food, and his kitchen cabinets never failed to have the latest snacks. I had my own room that I loved to lock myself in. It wasn't anything special. I had a 50' inch cable TV, a queen sized bed, and a window with a view of the house next door.

The room had a closet big enough to hold all of my belongings stuffed in black trash bags. I never liked to unpack and fold my clothes away. It was a habit of mine.

The only problem I had living with my uncle Derk was his buddy, Eric, who occasionally lived in the basement. I always felt extremely uncomfortable around him. There was always an awkward energy when he was around. He was an extremely short and stumpy older black man with a shiny bald head. He looked like a rotten milk dud with red dots for eyes. I always smelled him coming before I saw him. His clothes reeked of malt liquor and had several stains on them. The basement door was connected to the kitchen. I hated bumping into him on snack runs. I couldn't understand why my uncle befriended him.

One day I was home alone watching TV with my room door closed. I had enough snacks and juice for a binge watching session of my favorite dance competition show called *Bring It.* As soon as the theme music started playing, I snuggled deep underneath my covers. I didn't care about getting crumbs on my sheets.

The house was completely silent. The only thing I could hear was the sounds coming from my TV. Then, out of nowhere, I heard heavy footsteps creeping up the stairs. I just knew it was Eric, because no one else was home. But I had no idea where he was slithering too. If he had to use the bathroom there was one by the kitchen. Then all of a sudden, I heard him turning my doorknob.

"Hang on!" I shouted.

I tossed my blanket aside and jumped up. I leaped over and pressed my weight against the door. He was trying to come in.

"Go away!" I screamed.

He never responded to me. In fact, he never said any words. He just kept grunting, breathing heavy, and pressing against the door like an animal.

"Stop!" I screeched at the top of my lungs.

The door was the only thing keeping his grubby hands off me. He kept pushing and turning the knob. And I kept pressing back. After what seemed like the longest seven minutes of my life, he finally stopped. It was like a switch turned off in his head. Luckily, the flimsy hook lock and my 120 pound body were strong enough to keep me safe. I heard him stumble back downstairs. I didn't cry, or hop on the phone. I didn't call my dad, because I knew if I told him, he'd do something to land himself back in jail. I didn't call the police, because Eric didn't touch me. I didn't call my uncle Derk, because I didn't know what to say. I was too traumatized to open my door for the rest of the day. I kept the door locked and zoned out. Even when I was hungry or had to use the bathroom, I stayed in my room. I didn't come out of my room until uncle Derk came home hours later.

He sat down on the recliner sofa, extended the bottom and turned on the TV. I came downstairs slowly, and sat down on the stairs across from him.

"Hey, hey, hey," he said gleefully.

"Hey Uncle Derk," I replied softly. I felt myself tearing up, but I stopped.

"What's going on?" he asked.

I didn't talk often, but he could sense something was wrong with me.

I didn't waste any time and described everything that happened. To

7

my surprise, he seemed very unmoved by my story.

"He was probably just drunk," he said.

My heart broke into a million pieces. That was the moment when I lost all faith in my family.

"Yeah," I agreed.

I didn't continue wasting my breath after he said that. My uncle let Eric continue living there. I don't even think he confronted him about it. The next day came, and I just had to get over it. I later learned that the guy did the same thing to my uncle's daughter that used to live there. He tried to break into her room while drunk, and was unsuccessful. I didn't understand any of it, and I didn't want to. I had a boyfriend at the time. We're not together anymore, but back then I told him and his mom about what happened. Thankfully, his mom let me stay at their house for as long as I needed to. It felt like they cared more than my uncle did. The way he handled the situation hurt me, but I never told him. In fact, I never said much ever again. I just went back to being antisocial.

* * *

To cut a long story short, I lived with my friend Tanya that summer instead of my family. We met through a mutual friend in high school. She was a grade higher than me, and had a "mama bear" personality. I was drawn to that. We hung out a few times, but didn't become close right away.

She reached out to me about producing a talk show with her, after I graduated. She said she saw my posts on Facebook about interning with Fox 29 News and thought I might be interested. I thought it'd be a cool summer project to work on, and a great way to practice speaking in front of a camera. It was a no-brainer for me.

Tanya was hardworking, driven, and passionate about her work. Working on the show together with her, made me realize that she was the type of person that I could relate to. I probably spent every day at Tanya's house before I headed back to New York. Ms. Claire, Tanya's mom, embraced me too. She was so understanding and cared for me like her own daughter. It was like Tanya became my sister overnight. I never had the chance to bond with my own sister because we were separated growing up. But Tanya filled that void for me.

Her mom told me that I was more than welcome to stay with them anytime I wanted to. By this time, I couldn't stay at my ex-boyfriends house, because we had broken up. I couldn't stay with my dad, because he didn't have a steady place to live. I didn't feel protected living at my uncle's place anymore. And I wasn't close enough with any other family members to ask them. So I took a chance and asked Ms. Claire and Tanya if I could stay at their house during the summers. Thankfully, they said yes.

So whenever I came home from school I stayed with them. Everything was great, I got along with Ms. Claire, Tanya and her younger brother, Jim. I was looking forward to a summer with them. For a moment, I felt embraced and loved for the first time since my Grandma Harriet died.

Then the highlight of my summer happened.

It was just a normal day in Philadelphia. Tanya and I didn't have any plans so we stayed in. We watched a ton of Lifetime movies like we always did, and talked. I loved days like that with her. She told me about the fun family vacation experiences she's had in the past. I was amazed! The only real family vacation experience I had was traveling to the Poconos with my uncle Derk. But her family went on a big trip every single year. And that year they were vacationing in Orlando, a place where they had stayed numerous times before.

"Do you want to come with us this year?" she asked.

"Your family would let me come?" I replied hesitantly.

"Yeah, my aunt wouldn't mind you coming, she always gets a big condo to say in," she insisted.

"Okay, I would love to go, if it's cool with her," I smiled.

I was really excited, but I didn't want to show how much. She had loads of videos in her phone of her on cruises and different resorts, and cool restaurants with her favorite cousins, Angela and Amir. Angela was Tanya's younger cousin. But Tanya looked up to Angela as the older sister she never had. Amir was Angela's older brother, who Tanya adored as the older brother she never had. They had a beautiful bond that nobody could break.

I had never traveled with another family before, but hearing about all the fun they had on previous trips erased any fears. It seemed like everything in my life was starting to look up. I had an amazing friend with a welcoming family. I had a great internship for my dream job. On top of that, I attended my dream school on a full-tuition scholarship. Life felt really great.

Peace. The beginning of that summer was about finding peace in my life. I was starting to carve out my own slice of happiness in this world. For once, I didn't feel so out of place. It felt like I was right where I was supposed to be.

Lesson #1: You're a lot stronger than you think.

3

The City Beautiful

The trip was approaching faster than a New York Train. And I still needed to buy my plane ticket. My internship was my only source of income at the time. So I made sure I didn't miss any days of work, and even took extra jobs whenever I was free. Unfortunately, the ticket prices kept rising, and I wasn't scheduled to receive my paycheck anytime soon. Those moments were the ones I hated the most. I had a great opportunity in front of me, but no way to afford it.

"You bought your plane ticket yet?" Tanya asked.

We were sitting on her bed watching TV as usual.

I looked over and said, "No, not yet. I can't get it until I get paid."

Tanya made a face. I already knew what the face meant. I gave her a face too, and I'm sure she knew what mine meant – I'm broke.

"Oh ok, the prices are so cheap right now though," she replied.

"It'll be cheaper if you get it now," she continued.

"Yeah, I saw that, I hope they don't go up too much, there's nothing I can do until next week," I said picking up my phone to search for flights.

"Look, honestly, they are going to go up," Tanya warned.

"My mom can probably buy your ticket," she insisted.

"I don't know," I responded.

The ticket prices were incredible, but I felt like imposing on their trip was enough. I didn't want to add anything extra.

"I don't want her to have to do that," I continued.

"Ok, but if you keep waiting they're going to be too high. I'm telling you," Tanya warned.

"My mom is not going to mind paying for your ticket," she said.

"I'll think about," I replied.

It didn't take me long to come to my senses. I ended up asking Ms. Claire to buy my plane ticket. And I paid her back as soon as I got paid. Tanya and Ms. Claire always tried to make me feel comfortable asking for help. But it wasn't something I was used to. I was scarred after living with my crazy aunt Linda. That's where I stayed before I lived with my uncle Derek. I call her my crazy aunt, because she truly was at times.

I remember not being able to attend my 8th-grade school dance because I was "being disrespectful" about something she came up with. But it was really about the money. She just didn't want to buy

13

me a dress or pay for my dance ticket. She never wanted to spend any of her money on me. My school class still nominated me as "Dance Queen," although I wasn't there. When I told her about it I wanted her to feel bad for not letting me go. But she didn't care one bit.

The next year came, and her son went to the same school dance. And even had a big send off. She would always say, "I don't have any money for that," yet always made a way for him. When it came to her kids, especially her son, they went on every trip, to every dance, and got every sneaker. I had to watch it all, in my worn down shoes, and try my best to remain respectful. It was only so much a girl named Patience could tolerate. God didn't give me the gift of having two loving parents. But he gave me other gifts. And living with my crazy aunt Linda helped me unlock my passion for creative writing. I wrote down all of the things I wish I could have said to her.

I always appreciated her for taking me in after my Grandma Harriet died. I could have been homeless or sent to an orphanage. She didn't have to do that, and she always reminded me of it. But like Maya Angelou said, "people will forget what you said, people will forget what you did, but people will never forget how you made them feel." And I would have done anything to never have to feel like a burden ever again.

* * *

The vacation was the only thing that I day-dreamed about that summer. I envisioned the palm trees, and pictured myself gently grazing their trunks. Images of Orlando's tantalizing beaches, and magnificent waters pervaded my mind. I kept imagining myself lying on a beach unfazed by any worries back at home. I needed that dream to become my reality as much I needed to take my next breath.

Once I had my ticket, nothing was going to stop me from going. Which is why I didn't tell my dad. He would've been suspicious, and told me not to go. I didn't talk to my dad that often, but when I did Tanya and Ms. Claire always came up. My dad couldn't provide a roof over my head. And he definitely couldn't take me to Orlando, or pay for my plane ticket. He wanted to do more for me, but he couldn't. His prison record labeled him as threat to society, and the world doesn't forgive like a daughter does. I felt bad for him, so I left out a lot of things whenever we talked. The last thing I wanted to do was make him feel any worse.

But I also didn't want to worry about upsetting my dad either. I just wanted to have fun. And in the days leading up to the trip I was truly enjoying myself. Angela came over Tanya's house more often. I loved being around them. Those two had a heart-warming bond, and just listening to their jaw-dropping family stories entertained me.

I really wanted to get to know Angela on a personal level. All I knew was that she had a charismatic personality and played basketball, that was it. I never even got a chance to see her play. She was open to building a friendship with me, and didn't mind me being around. That was a huge relief for me. I was around Tanya all the time, and if Angela didn't like me that would have been weird. But she was always super nice to me.

The three of us started hanging out together. We went to the nail salon and did some last minute shopping a couple of days before the trip. I learned that we all had similar interests in fashion, hair, and nail art. I assumed that Angela wouldn't care for extravagant nails, or having the best hair, because she played basketball. But I was wrong, we had more in common than I thought. In fact, the nail design she picked out for vacation looked way better than mine.

But regardless of what my nail designs were, I was ready to leave. The thought of hopping on a plane for the first time electrified me.

My brain wouldn't stop drifting off. I barely got any sleep the night before we left. The next morning Tanya and I headed over to Angela's house. Her place was closer to the airport, so it made sense to leave from there. When Tanya and I got there Angela was home doing laundry and putting away leftovers. Well, most of it; we stuffed our faces with tacos that her mom, Ms. Nicole, made the night before. We didn't want to be hungry on the plane, and airport food couldn't have possibly tasted better than those tacos.

I didn't think Angela was going to finish her laundry in time. We were leaving in 20 minutes. And it was a huge white laundry basket filled to the brim with damp clothes in the living room.

Angela picked up a damp shirt and asked, "Y'all wanna help me hang some clothes?"

"Sure," Tanya replied.

"Yeah, no problem," I responded quickly.

Then suddenly, I remembered that I needed to grab some deodorant from the store. I wasn't wearing any, and I didn't want to ask anyone else for theirs. That would've been gross.

"My bad, I just remembered I have to run to the store real quick," I apologized.

"Oh ok, that's fine," Angela replied.

"Make sure you hurry up," Tanya added.

"My mom's on her way here," she said.

"Okay bet," I replied rushing out the door.

I felt bad that I couldn't help Angela hang clothes. But deodorant was a necessity for me, believe me. I power walked the ten minute distance to the store under the extremely hot weather. The temperature must have been upwards of 80 degrees. My hair was tied up into a ponytail, which helped a lot, but my forehead was on fire. The sun was relentless and my head hurt because I had a sew-in, and the braids underneath my ponytail were still extremely tight. Luckily, I wore jean shorts, a thin T-shirt, and open sandals to alleviate some of heat.

I finally reached the store. Of course, I grabbed more stuff than what I came for. Deodorant turned into hair ties, bobby pins, lip balm, and hair removal cream. I would have grabbed more, but I didn't want to take any more time. Ms. Nicole was on her way to pick us up and I wanted to make sure I was there before she arrived. Luckily, there were only a few people in line so I checked out pretty fast.

I made good time and power walked back to Angela's house in seven minutes or less. When I arrived, Ms. Nicole was just pulling up but I didn't see Ms. Claire with her. I walked in the house, and sat down on the couch.

I looked over at Tanya and Angela. They just finished hanging up the clothes.

"Where's your mom at?" I asked.

"She should be on her way now," Tanya replied.

"Ok good, I need to put this stuff in my suitcase," I said tying the tops of my plastic bags together. I sat them down next to my feet.

It wasn't long before Ms. Claire arrived. Once she did, everyone was ready to go. We had one car that was only big enough to fit our luggage. So Ms. Nicole decided to take us to the airport in groups. The first group included myself, Tanya, Angela and her younger sister Ayan. Once Ms. Nicole dropped us off, she went back for the others.

The four of us found a great spot to sit by the entrance. There was a huge window so we could see everyone else when they pulled up. It only took 20 minutes for us to fall asleep. Except for Angela, she was the only one who stayed awake surfing the web on her laptop.

I looked at her and said, "You have internet?"

I was puzzled.

She made a face, and rose her eyebrows a little.

"Yes," she smirked.

"Oh wow, that's dope," I replied naively.

To be fair, it was my first time in an airport. But I eventually realized that there was free WiFi available for everyone. I didn't realize that before. And to think, I attended NYU. I couldn't wait to redeem myself after asking her that dumb question.

Ms. Nicole finally returned with the second group 45 minutes later. It was Ms. Claire, Tanya's younger brother Jim, and Angela's father, Mr. Arthur. The only person missing was Amir. He already lived in Florida. So he planned on meeting us in Orlando once we got settled.

It didn't take us long to check our bags and head through security. The airport caught me by surprise. I didn't expect to see so many clothing stores, and fragrance boutiques. It felt like I was walking through a big mall. That made me even more curious to see Orlando. If the Philadelphia airport excited me, I knew that Florida would blow me away.

Things were moving exceptionally smooth. We boarded the plane and quickly found our seats without any problems. Except for one small one. I was seated in the middle of two strangers. Ms. Claire, Jim, and Tanya sat close by, but I was nervous. It was my first time on a plane. If something bad happened, I wanted to at least be sitting next to my friend. Tanya was in a middle seat like I was, in between Ms. Claire and Jim. So I figured that she might want to move as well.

I turned my head around and called her "Tee," everyone called her that for short.

"Yup," she responded from across the aisle.

"Do you want to see if we could sit together somewhere?" I whispered obnoxiously loud.

"Sure, I saw some empty seats in the back," she replied.

She stopped a female attendant that was passing by. I overheard her asking if she could move.

"Sure, that's not a problem," the female attendant said.

I quickly raised my hand. The female flight attendant walked over to me.

"Can I move too?" I asked sweetly.

"It's my first on a plane, and I just want to sit with my friend," I begged.

"Ok sure, go ahead," she responded.

"Thank you so much!" I smiled.

I didn't waste any time. I grabbed my neck pillow and scurried to the back. Tanya wanted the window seat, which was perfectly fine with me. I wanted to stretch my legs in the aisle anyway.

There was an extra seat in between us. We figured that Angela would want to sit with us too. So Tanya called her to the back of the plane.

"Angela!" she shouted.

"Angela!" she shouted again.

She couldn't hear, because she was wearing headphones.

"I'll just text her," Tanya said.

Angela must have gotten it, and started walking towards us. A flight attendant stopped her out of nowhere. We couldn't hear what their conversation was, but Angela turned around and went back to her seat. We were very confused. The flight attendant started walking in our direction so we stopped her.

"How come she can't sit with us too?" Tanya questioned.

"Well, we can't have too many people back here in this row, because it will throw off the weight of the plane," she replied.

I looked at Tanya and said, "Wow."

I never heard of anything like that before, I thought.

"That doesn't make any sense," Tanya argued.

She pointed at a row of empty seats across from us and asked, "She can't even sit over there?"

"No, I'm sorry," she said apologetically before walking away.

I was totally lost and didn't understand how adding one more person would have shifted the entire plane's weight balance. At the time, I thought it was a load of crap. But there was nothing we could do.

It was weird to see Angela in the front of the plane surrounded by a bunch of strangers. She was so far from her parents. But she didn't seem bothered by it. Angela just put her headphones on and zoned out to music. I liked her style, she always seemed unfazed.

* * *

Tanya fell asleep like a baby, but I couldn't. My head hurt too badly. I was so jealous of how comfortable she looked. Her head rested perfectly on an emoji themed neck pillow that she picked up during our shopping trip. She propped it up against the window for extra support. I instantly regretted not taking the window seat. Although I loved my aisle seat, I couldn't find a decent way to lay my head down. I had a neck pillow too. But it was stiffer than my environmental science professor. I tried laying my head on my bag, on Tanya's shoulder, my armrest, but nothing worked. No matter how hard I fought to fall asleep, I stayed up the entire flight. Thankfully, the flight was short so

I didn't suffer for too long.

As soon as the plane's tires scrapped against the ground, my heart skipped a beat. I had one goal, to get off the plane. I couldn't wait to smell Orlando's air and bask in its friendly sun. Tanya and I were all smiles. The energy was amazing; the vacation hadn't started yet, but it already felt legendary. We flew through the airport, eager to reach the vacation home. We were going to be living lavishly in paradise for an entire week! It was so surreal, all I could do was look at everything and take it all in.

We stopped for pizza since everyone was hungry. We sat down at a booth and waited for our orders to get ready. All I could do was examine the group of people that surrounded me. They were a loving, fun, and playful group, much different from the family members I encountered growing up. I was happy to be there, creating new memories with them.

I watched Angela and Jim crack jokes on each other left and right. The two of them should have had their own reality TV show. They were an amusing pair, and their jokes didn't stop once the food came. It only got more and more entertaining.

I just kept staring at everything, I didn't say much. I stared at Ayan stuffing her little chubby cheeks with pizza. I watched Ms. Claire go get a cup of coffee, and I watched and watched and watched. I wanted to get to know them, and not just be with them, but be a part of them. I had a chance to experience a real vacation, with a dope family. For me, the trip meant way more than touching palm trees. It was about finding a sense of belonging.

We couldn't wait to get on the road. But in order to get to the vacation home, we needed to get a rental car. In order to get a rental car, we needed to take a shuttle bus. So we went outside and looked for the right bus stop to stand in front of. There were several families waiting for buses as well. That's how we knew we were in the right place.

When I walked outside it felt like I put a sweater on. The humidity was so intense. I never felt anything like it. I was used to extreme heat, but extreme humidity was something entirely different. I wasn't in Philly any more, that was for sure.

I decided to create a new SnapChat account while waiting for the bus to arrive. I couldn't remember the login information for my old one, because I barely used it. Now I actually had a good reason to post on my snap.

When the first shuttle bus arrived, there wasn't enough room for all of us. So the adults decided to go ahead of us. Since they were paying for the rental car anyway, it made the most sense. It wasn't long before the next bus came. I hopped on and found a great window seat. I was in awe of Orlando, the palm trees were even more beautiful in person. I couldn't wait to touch them.

The ride was really short. It didn't take us long to arrive at the car rental place. We hopped off the bus and waited for the adults outside. The lines were extremely long, and it took forever to process paperwork. It was daylight when we got there, but we didn't leave until 10 pm.

We passed the time by dancing to party music. Angela kept replaying one of her favorite dance records. There were a series of intricate dance moves that accompanied the song. But Rhythm wasn't exactly my best-friend at the time. I couldn't figure out how to do any of the steps. Everyone else mastered them with no problem. Even Ayan had more rhythm than me, and she was only six years old. After failing over and over again, I finally decided to sit down on my suitcase.

Watching everyone else was more fun than embarrassing myself.

The time flew by, and before we knew it the adults were signaling us over to them. They rented two small cars. So we split into two groups again. Tanya, Jim, Ms. Claire and I were in one car, and Ms. Nicole, Angela, Ayan, and Mr. Arthur were in the other car. Ms. Claire noticed a couple of scratches on our rental car and made sure the rental place made note of it. But we were on the road in no time.

* * *

The day kept dragging along. Travel was more exhausting than I thought. It was around 12 am, and we still hadn't found the vacation home. We were close by according to the GPS, but we couldn't pinpoint where it was. Ms. Nicole called Ms. Claire and assured her that she knew where it was. She put us back on track within a few turns.

I was relieved, because I needed to use the restroom so bad. I didn't want to slow everyone down, but I had to go. Holding it in until we got there wasn't an option.

"Ms. Claire, can you stop somewhere real fast? I have to use the bathroom so bad," I said.

"Yeah sure that's not a problem," she answered.

She pulled over at a McDonald's, and let Ms. Nicole know we took a bathroom break. It was a quick mission, we were back on the road in 5 minutes or less. After passing a few restaurants we pulled into a complex. Apparently, the house was a part of a town home community. That explained our difficulty of finding it.

We parked and started getting out one by one.

"This is nice," Ms. Claire said.

"Yes I love this," Ms. Nicole added.

The home was very charming, its landscape was simply picturesque. Slender palm trees and tiny lizards decorated the front of the house. I caressed the bark of a palm tree with the palm of my hands. I grazed my fingers over its ridges, while taking a deep breath, and inhaling the air. I exhaled and smiled.

"This is amazing," I whispered.

The tree didn't give me any supernatural abilities, but it made me feel special.

The house was more breathtaking on the inside. Although the living room, dining room, and kitchen were in the same room, everything was spread out perfectly. The living room had couches, a coffee table, and a huge TV. The kitchen was spotless. It was the neatest kitchen I had ever seen. There were hand towels folded into heart-shaped doves on the counter top.

"This is just too cute," I said. I had never seen hand towels used as decoration before. I thought it was brilliant. I took a picture of the design so I could learn how to re-create it later.

"I'm about to go claim my room," Tanya announced.

I followed behind her. We claimed the first room we saw. It was right by the kitchen, and was perfect for us. There were two twin beds, and a spacious closet to hide our luggage.

Ms. Claire and Angela playfully fought over one of the larger rooms.

They didn't want to share the space.

"Oh no, you can't have this room," Angela joked.

"What do you mean? I helped pay for this," Ms. Claire laughed.

"So, I already put my bag in there," Angela said.

She put her arm against the wall so Ms. Claire couldn't walk by.

"Oop," Ms. Claire shouted.

"Girl, you better move," she laughed.

I was captivated by their fun-loving relationship. Angela had enough material to crack jokes on Ms. Claire all night.

Everyone settled into their selected spaces. Angela eventually surrendered and claimed the pull-out couch with Jim. Angela's parents were in the master suite all to themselves. And I had no idea where Amir was going to sleep. He was driving up to meet everyone the next day. I figured that he was going to sleep in the living room with Angela and Jim.

I opened up my suitcase, but didn't unpack any clothes. I was completely worn out. My eye lids felt like mini blankets that warmed me up whenever I closed them. Everyone else was too excited to sleep right away, and decided to watch a movie. I didn't want to be a party pooper, but I was ready for bed. I wanted to watch the movie with them, I really did. But my eyes would not stay open. I knew that we had an entire week together, so I called it a night.

* * *

The next day came like a pleasant surprise. The sun peaked through our window, and kissed my forehead. I slowly opened my eyes, and was taken aback for a moment. I almost forgot that I was in Orlando. It was refreshing to wake up somewhere so delightful. Tanya and I sat up.

"I wonder what we're going to do today," I said.

"Girl, it's so much stuff we can do," she laughed.

"Oh my god, I can't wait," I squealed.

We got up, and walked into the kitchen. Everyone else began waking up one after another. Ms. Claire came into the living room.

"Mom, what are we going to first?" Tanya asked.

"Oh I don't know, but I'm hungry," she said sitting down.

"I'm just ready to get out of this house," Tanya replied.

"Me too, but I have to grab a bite to eat first," Ms. Claire said shaking her head.

We were eager to do something fun, but there wasn't any food in the house. Ms. Nicole came into the living room.

She grabbed her keys and said, "We're about to go to the grocery store now."

"Oh okay, I'm coming with y'all then," Ms. Claire responded.

"Can I go too?" I asked desperately wanting to see outside.

"Yeah come on, were all going to go," Ms. Claire said.

Angela and Jim stayed behind. They must've stayed up all night watching that movie. Everyone else piled into the rental cars. The adults decided to make it one big shopping trip. Just so there would be plenty of food in the house for the entire week.

We pulled up to a gigantic Walmart, and then the cart wars began. Ms. Claire had a cart, and Angela's parents had their own cart. They were filling up quickly. A variety of frozen foods, chips, and drinks were tossed in left and right. It was almost like they were competing to see who could grab the most stuff. I never seen shopping carts so packed in my entire life.

"I'm making chicken and shrimp alfredo tonight," Ms. Nicole said.

My heart dropped into my shoes.

"Oh my god," I whispered.

"What?" Tanya asked.

"That is my favorite dish," I smiled.

I wanted to cry, because I was so ecstatic.

"This girl is so fat," Tanya laughed.

The vacation was off to an exceptional start. Tanya's family had the type of energy to make a trip to the supermarket gratifying. Once we grabbed everything we needed, we stood in line. It took a while to check out. The lines in Walmart were super long. And we had several items to scan. I couldn't wait to leave, just so Ms. Nicole could start making the pasta. I knew that she wasn't making it just for me. But I felt like the stars were aligning in my favor.

When we returned eager to unload the goods. I grabbed a handful of bags and headed inside. When I opened the door Angela was stretched out on the sofa bed watching a movie. Jim was on the other couch on his phone. And little Ayan was walking around with her toys.

"You need help with that?" Jim asked.

He hopped up from the couch and walked over to me.

"There's plenty of bags in the car," I joked.

"Haha okay," he said slipping his shoes on.

Jim helped us bring the rest of the bags inside. There were a bunch of them. Thankfully, everyone joined forces to help store the food away. So it didn't take too long.

Tanya and I were ready to dig in. She tossed a couple of pieces of Italian sausage in the skillet and started making breakfast for us. She loved to cook, and was always willing to teach me a thing or two. Everyone else decided to make sandwiches until Ms. Nicole made the pasta. Tanya and I went into our room after we ate.

We didn't want to stop talking about all the fun we were going to have. But somehow, we fell asleep. We didn't plan on taking a nap, but I was happy we did. I was still recovering from the flight and driving fiasco.

By the time we woke up Ms. Nicole was almost finished cooking dinner.

Angela came into the room and chatted with us. Angela couldn't wait for Amir to get there. she said the real fun was going to start when he got there. Just like her, he was the life of every party. We were so excited about the future of the trip. There was no way we were staying in the house all day. We talked about going on a cruise, seeing a magic show, and exploring Universal Studios. The possibilities were endless.

Dinner was finally ready. Ms. Nicole made a HUGE pot of delicious chicken and shrimp alfredo. It smelled like heaven, I could barely hold my excitement in. She was a little upset because she forgot to buy Obay Seasoning. But no one thought it made a big difference. Especially not me. I sat down with a huge smile.

It felt good to be sitting at the table with everyone. Just watching how they all interacted with one another was enjoyable. It was hilarious listening to Angela and Jim crack more jokes on each other. I couldn't believe they hadn't run out of comebacks yet. The entire experience was beautiful.

Everyone went back to relaxing after dinner. Me, Tanya, and Angela slowly returned to the room. We decided to have a girl talk. Tanya told us about this new guy she met and asked us for advice. She didn't know if she should take him seriously.

"You should just have fun right now," I said.

"Yeah, it's nothing wrong with going on date," Angela added.

"Yeah I guess," she replied.

It was cool to hang with the girls chatting it up about boys, clothes, and whatever else came to mind. We slowly drifted away from that conversation and started admiring each other's new outfits. I unloaded my suitcase on the bed. There were so many fashionable choices I picked out. I couldn't wait to try them on.

* * *

It was the late evening, but the sun was still shining bright. I couldn't believe that we were still inside. I could have sat in the house in Philadelphia, but we were in Orlando. And it was no telling when I was going to get an opportunity to come back. So I told the girls about an event I heard promoted on the radio during the driving fiasco. I assumed it was going to be worthwhile, because the event ad played during every commercial break.

"I think it's going to be fun!" I begged.

"I don't know about that," Tanya mumbled.

"Yeah," Angela added.

I searched for the flyer on Instagram until I found it. It was a music event being held at a nightclub in downtown Orlando. The headliner was supposed to be a big local rapper. I loved music events, so I was sold. But the girls weren't at all.

"But we're not 21," Angela said.

"Yeah I don't want to get all dressed up, and then have to come right back," Tanya added.

"Yeah, that makes sense," I agreed.

I was slightly disappointed, because I really wanted to go that event. But they were right, it wasn't like we were home. Angela started googling 18 and up clubs in Orlando. The only thing we had to worry about was the admission price.

"This one looks lit," Angela said.

"Let me see," Tanya replied and grabbed the phone.

"Oh ok, I like this," she smiled.

"Let me see," I whined and then walked over to them.

"Oh snap that's crazy," I said.

The pictures were enticing, and it was only a 35-minute drive away. On top of that, there were so many great reviews.

"I think it's a gay nightclub," Tanya said.

"Yeah," I added.

"Oh okay, I mean, I don't care," Angela said.

"Shoot me neither! I'm about to beat my face to the Gods, hunny," Tanya laughed.

"Yes! Oh my god, we HAVE to slay tonight," I added.

"Yes!" Tanya shouted.

"Y'all going to be all cute and stuff," Angela whined.

"Tee you going to do my make up?" she asked.

Tanya sucked her teeth and said, "Girl, you know I was going to do your make up."

"You think we should call them?" I asked.

"Yeah we should still call," Tanya replied.

"I'm about to call now," Angela said.

None of us went to a gay nightclub before. I only knew what I saw on TV. I pictured fabulous drag queens with the best makeup, voluminous hair, and sparkly glitter everywhere. I was looking forward to the experience. And we figured that a gay nightclub would be more entertaining than anywhere else.

Ms. Nicole heard us chattering and came in the room.

"What y'all in here shouting about?" she questioned.

"We're about to go out," Angela replied.

"Yesss," Tanya and I celebrated in unison.

"Where y'all going to go?" Ms. Nicole asked.

Angela showed her the phone and said, "This place called Pulse, it's in downtown Orlando."

"And how do y'all think you're getting there?" she laughed.

That was actually a great question. We didn't consider how we were getting there yet.

"We could take an Uber," Tanya suggested.

"Yeah, we could split it," I added.

"Oh I don't know," Ms. Nicole said hesitantly.

"It's already so late," she said sitting down at the edge of my bed.

"Well, I am a little tired," Angela said.

"But I don't feel like staying in the house either," she added.

"Yes, come on get dressed," Tanya replied.

"Better yet, I have to start your makeup anyway," she said reaching for her suitcase.

Ms. Claire heard the noise and stood in the doorway.

"What's going on in here?" she asked.

"They talking about going out," Ms. Nicole answered.

"It's late isn't it?" Ms. Claire said raising her eyebrows.

"Mom, the club don't start getting lit until 12am," Tanya argued.

"How y'all getting there?" Ms. Claire questioned.

"We were going to uber," Tanya replied.

"Me and Arthur probably will end up taking them," Ms. Nicole interjected.

"Oh my God yes," Angela celebrated.

"We lit!" Tanya shouted.

"I'm about to start doing my makeup!" I squealed.

Ms. Nicole and Angela called the club to make sure our age wouldn't be a problem. We didn't want to have any surprises that night. They found out we were good to go, and that the admission price was only ten dollars.

"Only ten bucks!" I celebrated.

Having fun in Orlando was way cheaper than Philadelphia. We spent a lot of time dramatizing our makeup, but it didn't take us too long to get ready. Tanya did Angela's makeup to perfection, while I struggled to do my own. I sat on the floor in front of the closet mirror concentrating intensely. I was accustomed to Tanya doing my makeup. She was the makeup artist, not me. I could never give myself that extra pop like she could. But there wasn't enough time for her to do Angela's face, and mine. Angela was so lucky.

"What are you doing to your eyebrows?" Angela questioned.

"I'm just cleaning them up with concealer," I said trying to sound makeup educated.

"I'm not as good as Tanya, so I have to clean them up," I added.

"Oh ok, they look nice though" Angela replied.

"Aww thank you, I'm trying," I laughed.

"Tanya always does my make up," I added.

"Yeah that's why I had to teach her a few things," Tanya said cleaning one of her brushes.

"I'm not always going to be able to do it, so she had to learn," she continued.

Tanya finished Angela's makeup and her own. We got dressed, and took some selfies before heading out. Ms. Nicole and Mr. Arthur did end up driving us. Angela and I stayed awake the whole ride, but Tanya fell asleep ten minutes in. We didn't really talk the whole ride. Angela texted on her phone the whole time. Her cellphone was blowing up with notifications. I was super nosy, and ended up noticing that her phone was dying.

"What kind of iPhone do you have?" I asked.

"Oh, I got the 6," she replied.

She was talking about the iPhone 6.

"Oh ok, you can use my case to charge your phone if you want," I offered.

"Ok bet, thanks," she said.

I handed her my pink Mobi charger case. She didn't have anywhere to put her phone case /cardholder.

"I can hold your stuff in my purse," I said.

"Thank you," she said handing me her belongings.

I know it wasn't much, but I was happy that I could do something nice for her. And redeem myself from that stupid WiFi question.

* * *

We arrived at Pulse Nightclub around 12 am. We thanked Angela's parents and hopped out.

"Do you guys have any cash?" I asked.

"Nope, we should probably go to an ATM, before we get inside," Tanya said.

"Yeah, I think they said cash at the door," Angela added.

Luckily for us, there was a 7-eleven right across the street. I decided to grab a pack of gum and get ten dollars in cash back instead of using the ATM. Tanya and Angela did the same. We were headed to back to Pulse in no time.

As soon as we walked out the store the energy shifted. We went from being slightly tired to dripping with anticipation. We were smiling and laughing just thinking about how much fun we were about to have. The music became clearer as we moved closer.

"Oh, they playing Usher!" I celebrated.

"Yessss," Tanya cheered.

We were only a few feet away from the door when I spotted a girl wearing the cutest boots I had ever seen. I could barely see what she looked like, but I saw her shoes a mile away. They were money print with a sharp stiletto heel. I was wearing sandals that I got from a clearance section. It didn't take much to impress me. And I was sure that people would have on more fabulous shoes inside for me to adore.

We reached finally reached the door. There was a charming lady behind the desk, and two women standing side by side checking ids. The woman behind the desk was super friendly, and she had a smile that could brighten anyone's day.

"Hello Ladies, Welcome," she smiled.

Her teeth were extremely white. We greeted her back, and smiled.

I never experienced that kind of hospitality at a nightclub before. In Philadelphia, people usually frowned at the door. But Pulse nightclub was different. The women asked to see our IDs, so we handed them over. They checked them and looked up at us.

"You're good," one of the women said.

The vibrant lady at the front desk smiled and said, "It'll be 10 dollars."

Before I could reach into my purse, the girl I spotted with the really cute boots tapped me.

"Hey if you want, you can be my plus one so you don't have to pay," she offered.

I was stunned.

"My friends didn't show up," she continued.

"Oh my god, thank you so much!" I squealed.

I couldn't stop smiling.

"I was just saying how much I loved your boots!" I added.

"Haha, oh my gosh, it's no problem at all, why spend your money when I have a free ticket, you know?" she said handing it to me.

I was elated, that was the nicest thing a complete stranger ever did for me. I was finally able to take a good look at her. She wore black glasses, had beautifully cut bangs.

"Thank you so much! What's your name by the way?" I asked.

"Really, it's no problem, and I'm Emily," she said extending her hand.

"Well, Hi Emily, I'm Patience!" I replied.

"It's very nice to meet you," she smiled.

After paying we walked inside. There was nothing but positive energy flowing throughout the club. There was a stage with colorful flashing lights, and booming speakers. People didn't usually dance out in the open at Philadelphia clubs. Everyone would stand against the wall, or find a corner to hide in. But no one was afraid of dance floor in Pulse. Everyone was smiling and dancing without a care in the world. Pulse nightclub was a secret world that we tapped into. And the club goers were like a breath of fresh air.

Emily offered to buy us drinks out of nowhere.

"Thank you so much!" We squealed.

"You're welcome, ladies!" she replied.

"Let's have fun!" she shouted.

We cheered and started showing off some moves. The night was off to an exceptional start. It was better than I could've ever imagined.

I leaned over to Emily and asked, "Where are you from?"

"I'm from Pennsylvania," she replied.

"We're from Philly!" We screamed in unison.

We totally freaked out.

"No way!" she yelled.

"Yes we're from Philadelphia, Pennsylvania! That's so crazy!" I shouted.

"It's a small world," she smiled.

"Yes," Tanya added.

"So small," Angela said.

The performances began to start as we were standing by the bar. The hosts came onto the stage in their lavish outfits, and greeted us with their bold voices. They introduced the first performer, and told us to expect to see Beyoncé. As soon as they walked off, an electrifying woman entered the room singing passionately. I cheered at the top of my lungs. I couldn't believe how gorgeous she was. Her makeup was flawless, her outfit was magical, and her hair was fierce! I was mesmerized by all of the sparkly gems reflecting off of the lights. She knew how to engage a crowd, and added in some high-powered dance moves that brought the Beyoncé character to life. I couldn't believe that I was witnessing something so marvelous for free.

Emily leaned into our group and said, "I'm going to use the bathroom."

"Ok cool," I replied.

She walked off into the busy crowd.

I pulled out my phone and started recording the show. I was so happy that I made a new Snapchat account.

At the end of the performance, the hosts came back onto the stage. They started picking people from the audience asking them to come up for a dance battle. I tried not to make eye contact, because I didn't want to go up there. Watching the show was perfectly fine with me.

We met some more exciting people while enjoying the show. A group of guys came over and started talking to us.

One of them stood in front of me and said, "You almost made me forget I was gay for a second."

I was so taken aback that I almost spilled my free drink.

"Haha, stop it!" I giggled.

"I'm serious, you are gorgeous!" he shouted.

"Oh my god, thank you!" I replied.

I was so flattered and couldn't help but laugh. That was the last thing I expected him to say when he came over to me. The entire group of guys were super sweet and extremely well dressed. It was clear that they paid attention to detail. Their shoes were clean, and polished. And blew my little clearance sandals out of the water. And on top of that their eyebrows were a lot sharper than mine.

After the show was over, we decided to check the bathroom for Emily. She was gone for a long time. When we looked she wasn't in there. I decided to use the restroom anyway. She must have drifted off with her friends, I thought.

"Let's go see what else they have in here," Tanya suggested.

"Yeah it looks like a part back here," I said pointing to the back of the club.

"I think that's the music we heard outside," Angela added.

We walked through the entrance, and felt like we were in a brand new club.

"Yooo," I said.

It was a tropical patio, with its own bar, and DJ. They played reggae music instead of the pop we listened to inside. It was definitely more my speed. We ran into Emily again.

"Hey guys!" she shouted.

"Hey! We were looking for you!" I laughed.

"Oh sorry," she smiled.

It was no hard feelings, she was having a great time, and so were we. We started doing our best version of dutty wining, and wore ourselves out. The patio area had the best vibes, but no air conditioning. After a while, it became so hot that we decided to go back inside.

I hugged Emily and said, "See you!"

"It was so nice meeting you!" she replied.

"It was nice meeting you too, have a great night!" I yelled.

"You too!" she said blowing a kiss at me.

I smiled and walked inside. That was the last time I saw Emily that night.

We walked back to the first bar, and stood in our old spot. Angela spotted another section of the club. It was in the front of the club, and called the Adonis room. We saw people walking through the door, and heard the sounds of our favorite songs creeping out.

"We're definitely going in there," Angela said.

"Yesss let's go," Tanya added.

"Whoot! Whoot!" I cheered.

As soon as we walked through the door the fun began. We met a ton of new people and danced with them. There were even stripper poles that people could dance on for fun. Angela shocked us by being first to dance on one in front of everyone. We recorded her as she smiled and danced her heart out. It was so heart-warming to watch. She was having so much fun. When she hopped down, and a security guard came over to us.

"Hey you can't be on the poles," he said.

"Oh my bad," Angela laughed.

"We thought they were for everyone," I joked.

Tanya laughed really hard and said, "Right, it was just - right here."

The security guard wasn't upset, he was very friendly.

"Yeah I know, people do it all the time, but they're not supposed to," he smiled.

"Oh okay we'll stay off them," Tanya said.

We already took a great video of Angela, so we didn't care. He walked away, and we kept enjoying ourselves. Club goers started joining our little circle. I put my phone in my purse and started finding my rhythm. Angela and I danced together for the first time.

"Heyyy," I celebrated.

"Heyyy," she replied.

We were killing it. Tanya pulled out her phone started recording. Then people we didn't know started recording us too. Our mini performance was drawing a crowd. Her energy, and my energy blended perfectly. Angela was so much fun to be around. I saw a completely different side of her that night. And I was touched that she felt comfortable enough to unwind around me. It felt like we were finally bonding, and I couldn't be happier.

We took a break to catch our breath, and stood by the bar. There was a cute bartender that we flirted with. We knew he was gay, but it was fun to joke around with him anyway. I felt like I was inside an episode of Girlfriends. Of course I was Joan, Tanya was Tony, and Angela was Lynn.

"Yo, we have to come back here!" I shouted.

"Yesss!" Tanya yelled.

"This going to be our spot for the whole vacation!" Angela added.

"Oh my God, this is going to be so lit!" I screamed.

"Ahhh!" We cheered in unison.

The energy was mythical, no other outing compared to the fun I had with them. Tanya and Angela were the best friends anyone could have. They made a night out to the club, a once and a lifetime experience. I didn't want the night to end, but I knew it had to.

Lesson #2: Appreciate life while you still can.

4

The Last Pulse

I couldn't understand how things changed so quickly. The three of us were trapped inside of a bathroom. We were just dancing and laughing together. Then all of a sudden, we were screaming and scrambling around on a cold floor.

I felt bodies squirming around underneath me. I was on top of a pile of 15-20 people. The shooter fired endless rounds of bullets down at us. It felt like we had been herded together for slaughter. Until a miracle happened. Out of nowhere, the shooter shouted, "Damn, My gun's jammed!" I was relieved, terror-stricken, but relieved.

I turned to Tanya and said, "Let's bumrush him," but before we could even think about devising a plan to effectively do that the gunshots started again. I felt prickly pebbles popping against my legs. My mind wanted to believe they were pellets of a BB gun. I wanted to believe that it was all a joke or some sort of extended performance. I wanted to believe that we had left already.

But I looked down at my leg and saw a hole the size of a penny pouring red streams of blood. That didn't come from a pellet. It came from a venomous bullet that ripped through my flesh and bone. It became clear that the prickly pebbles I felt against my legs were actually tiny pieces of wall fragments flying everywhere. I shoved my phone in my bra and started to brace my leg.

Then, the gunfire stopped.

I wiggled and found a tight space on the floor next to someone. The pressure surrounding the bullet wound was awfully heavy. It felt like a boulder dropped on my leg and crushed it. It stunned my entire body. I kept trying to figure out when my dream warped into a nightmare. I looked around and tried to grasp the moment.

I saw the shooter's feet underneath the stall. I focused on the machine gun he had. My eyes were riveted to its long black frame. It was the first time I saw a machine gun in person. I only witnessed them in the movies. That's what it felt like I was in, a horror film.

I opened my mouth to speak.

"I've been shot," I whispered. It was a meager airy mumble. Nevertheless, hearing my own voice was enough to let me know that I was still alive. Streams of tears started flowing down my face faster than the blood pouring out of my wound. Raging aches were proliferating throughout my body. My fear intensified with each breath I took. I was alive but petrified at the fact that I could be shot again, and again, and again until I wasn't. My body couldn't handle any more torment, but my soul wasn't prepared to die.

We were all hurt, panicking, and processing. Some people were brave enough to get back on their phones and make calls to 911, and family members. I heard them desperately trying to get out crucial information despite their pain. Angela was one of those people.

I lifted my head from the floor and saw her with her phone raised to her ear as she braced her bleeding arm. she said, "please come get us, please, I'm shot!" Her voice sounded different, it was overburdened with agony. I saw sides of Angela I never knew existed. The girl that was once unfazed by everything, was begging for her life. I had seen her quiet, I had seen her laugh, I had seen her dance, and now I saw her cry. I wanted to get to know her more personally, but not in the way the universe created. I didn't want to see her break. I didn't want to see her wounded. I didn't want us to die. I desperately hoped Angela's calls would save us all. I took deep breaths and concentrated on staying calm.

The shooter stopped making noises. I didn't hear his voice, or his footsteps prowling back and forth. We were in the eye of the storm. He must have left the bathroom. It was a brief moment of silence. Some people used that time to make more calls. I heard wave after wave of cries to parents and to loved ones. I heard echoing sounds of busy dial tones beeping because too many called 911 at once.

The pain of my leg paralyzed me. I couldn't move. I wanted to call my dad, but I didn't know what to say. I didn't understand what was happening, or why it was happening. He was going to want answers that I couldn't give him. I just stayed there, bleeding out, waiting for death to find me.

The shooter returned and said, "Get off your phones."

He didn't yell or raise his voice. He said it peacefully. His demeanor didn't measure up to his monstrous behavior. He sounded like a regular guy. He sounded like I could have walked passed him on the street. And that was the most disturbing detail of all.

People began pleading to the shooter, begging him profusely to let us go. Angela mustered up enough courage to speak to him directly on behalf of everyone.

"Please just let us go! We won't say anything, just let us go!" she yelled bracing her bleeding arm.

He didn't respond to her or anyone. He paced back and forth holding his gun.

"Don't be stupid," he warned.

We tried to remain quiet. All of us. We didn't want to set him off in any way. We had been lying in each other's blood for several minutes, maybe an hour even. I felt my body getting weaker. My eyes wanted to shut, but I didn't know if they would open again.

The shooter stayed quiet for a while. Then out of nowhere, he broke the silence with a bizarre call to 911. He told the dispatcher that he was responsible for what was happening at Pulse.

"This is Isis," he said self-composed.

He wasn't shooting out of anger, he was shooting out of purpose. Any ounce of hope I had lingering in my heart was gone. I heard frightening details about Isis on the news and saw vicious beheading videos online. I never thought I'd be in the same room with one of their militant's. And I never thought I'd be afraid to be an American. He advised the police to stay away. I heard him say he had enough bombs to blow up a city block if they tried to make a move. Now I didn't know whether my life was going to end by another bullet or an explosive.

Before getting off the phone with 911 he spoke in another language pledging his allegiance to Isis. But then he quickly made another call.

A call no one could fully understand. It seemed as if he was talking to someone who helped him coordinate the attack. He told the person on the phone that he knew the police were going to try to come in, and if they did, he had enough bullets for them. He even mentioned that he was one of four shooters that night. I remember him saying verbatim "don't worry I got the snipers outside," before ending the call. I know the shooter did not work alone. Anyone alive in the bathroom to hear his calls know it too.

* * *

Time kept going past.

My body, from the neck down, was in the stall with Tanya and Angela. But I placed my face under the stall next to us. I was fearful that the gunman would enter our stall and shoot me in the face. However, the sight I witnessed underneath the other side would haunt me for the rest of my life. Lifeless bodies, drenched in each other's blood, just thrown on top of each other.

There was pure red blood smeared across the bottom of the toilet bowl. I tried to pull slide myself forward by grabbing onto the toilet bowl leaving my fingerprint marks. But I couldn't move from that position because my right leg was bent and pinned underneath the man right next to me. In agony, I slowly turned around, looked him in his eyes, and begged in a whisper "please get off my... leg it's been shot," he whispered back "I can't... it hurts, I'm sorry." He was also injured, so he couldn't move much either. I shed a few tears before turning my head back underneath the neighboring stall. Out of nowhere I felt a hand rubbing my arm trying to console me. I didn't know whose hand it was, nevertheless I appreciated that hand so much.

Phones kept ringing and receiving notifications every few minutes. Each time a phone went off, the shooter got more agitated and said "give it up," not saying what he would do if we didn't. But we all knew he would start shooting again.

A phone kept ringing, and no one stopped it. My stomach dropped onto the floor. I couldn't figure out where the sound was coming from. No one still alive could either. I tapped a man's arm slumped over the toilet praying it was his but they shook his finger at me saying it wasn't. I wanted to cry out and plead for mercy, but the shooter's frustration grew quickly because no one threw a phone out yet. I heard him pacing abruptly as if he was about to make a move. I could see his feet right outside of our stall door. I didn't want to die at that moment -I wanted life. I wanted to have hope. I was so scared that he would start shooting at us again that I reached into my bra, grabbed my phone, and threw it out to him.

I held my breath…hoping that it would satisfy him. The room was silent. It must have been an act of God because no other phones went off after I had thrown my phone out.

Time kept going past

I was losing hope. Each time I heard him click his gun, I lost more hope. Each time I heard him speak I lost even more hope. I was giving up…I actually felt myself giving up.

It was quiet in our bathroom, but suddenly he said to us "Are there any black people in here?" I wasn't sure if I should answer. I thought he might shoot me if I did.

Someone else responded to him saying "Yes there are about six or seven of us."

"You know.... I don't have a problem with black people, you guys have suffered enough, but I'm doing this for my country," he said.

"Did you hear about that Charleston shooting? That was horrible..." he continued.

I couldn't make sense of why he asked us those questions or why he said these things, but he said them. He stayed quiet for a while after that.

Time kept going past.

We were bleeding for hours, crying for hours, and fearful for hours. At times I felt a hand tapping my legs — it was Tanya checking to see if I was still alive. I raised my hand a little to show her I was. I didn't hear Angela's voice anymore. I hadn't heard it for a while.

There were just long periods of silence that made me want to find peace within myself. There were long moments of silence that made me want to die. Not knowing if I was going to make it out again. Laying in excruciating pain for hours made me beg God to take the soul out of my body. It makes you pray, and ask God to forgive you for any wrongdoing. It makes you regret not saying all the things you wanted to tell people, and extremely grateful for the things that you did say. The silence convinces you that you lived enough, so if you die now, you can die in peace and accept it. We were all hopeless and silent.

Suddenly there was a loud boom!

The entire building shook, all of us jolted in shock. Then there was another loud boom! Even louder than the first. I just knew it was the shooter activating his bombs. I knew that this was it, I was about to die.

I placed my hand near my mouth and clenched my fist in preparation for death. Then suddenly, there was another loud boom! I could see the shooter's feet scurrying in a panic, maybe it wasn't his bombs I thought. His feet moved closer, and closer to our stall.

Then out of nowhere, a voice over a speaker shouted: "Get Away from the walls!"

He ran into our stall. I felt his presence inches away from me. I was so scared all over again, my peace was gone.

His calm voice shook the room.

"Hey you," he said right before he shot someone.

POW! He immediately shot someone else. It was like he was going down a line. Then there was a lighting fast pause...where I felt the person right next to me get closer, I felt their body pressed on my arm, and then POW! He shot again. I heard the man on top of me scream inside my ear — he had been hit.

Then BOOM!

The wall came crashing down. The debris covered my face completely, although I could see through some of it. There was a light shining through the wall.

"Put down your weapon!" the police shouted.

"Put down your weapon down now!" they shouted once more.

A split second later all I heard was gunfire being exchanged between the shooter and the police. The bathroom lit up with sparks like a night sky on July 4th. Then there was nothing. For a moment there was silence.

This silence didn't terrify me, this new silence gave me hope again. I started crying, and asking the question "Is it over?" repeatedly out loud. I heard the police shouting and asking questions to us. My face was still covered with debris, and the stall wall that I had placed my face under was now pinned on top of me. I couldn't move much without being in pain. All of a sudden, I started feeling the slightly warm water rising quickly. I felt it rising past my ear which was on the ground. I started to panic, I thought I was going to drown if I didn't get from under all the rubble. I started squirming frantically and trying to push the stall wall from over the top of me. At first, I couldn't move it, then I started squealing in panic. The water was up to my cheek now, so I focused and pushed as hard as my body would allow. In a few grunts, I was able to lift it up enough to swiftly slide from underneath it.

I sat up and witnessed the full horror scene. Bodies all over, debris scattered over the top of them, bloody water rising up fast. The light was dim, It even looked like it may have been a red light. I slowly moved my leg from underneath the fallen hero that laid next to me. I looked around the bathroom, and I saw Tanya holding Angela across her lap and a black man who seemed to be unharmed communicating with the police.

Tanya's body and face were splattered with blood, her hair was wild, and her eyes were open very wide.

I asked her, "Are you shot?"

"Yes in my side," she replied.

Tanya started to cry and ask for help with Angela. When I realized Angela wasn't responding at all I lost it.

"What's wrong with Angela?" I cried.

"What's, what's wrong with Angela?" I stammered.

The black man in the stall with us, who was unharmed, went over to Angela and checked her pulse.

"She's still breathing, she still has a pulse!" he said.

That calmed us both down. I also couldn't handle the thought of thinking she was dead in that moment because I would've never left the floor. I would've stayed there crying with Tanya hysterically until I bled to death as well. Once he said that Angela was breathing that's when I started to pay attention to the police officers that were trying to talk to us.

The police shouted a number of questions "Is there any other gunman inside?! Are there any bombs inside?!" Those of us who were still conscious said that it was only one gunman in our bathroom and that there were no bombs. However, we warned the police in a panic that the gunman had snipers outside. They didn't really acknowledge us saying that they just ordered us to raise our hands above our heads. We didn't keep warning them because they must have already handled them — so we thought.

The police came through the hole in the wall. I remember looking up at the police officer with his helmet and a machine gun in his hand. I was in total disbelief. He shouted at me "Can you get yourself up?!" I didn't know yet. I hadn't tried to stand in three hours. When I attempted to, sharp pains shot through my entire body.

"I can't get up!" I cried out.

I couldn't, and each time I tried to pull myself up it felt like I was ripping my leg apart. I never felt a pain so intense before in my life.

The police officer said, "You have to try to push yourself up!"

I kept trying but I just couldn't get up. I was still sitting there. The police officer was right in front of me, I was saved, but I couldn't even reach him. I was more frustrated at how weak and hopeless I felt than anything.

Suddenly, I heard Tanya's voice pushing me to rise from the floor, "You're going to have to get up!" she screamed at me.

"I can't!" I cried back to her.

"You're going to get up and walk!" she screamed one final time.

Her voice rang in my ear, I don't know why but her words encouraged me more than ever before, giving me a strength I didn't know I had. Even in a moment where she was holding her dying cousin — with a bullet in her side — she still found a couple of seconds to be a friend to me.

I tried one more time, this time putting all my weight on my left leg, grabbing onto the falling stall wall and clenching my teeth through the sharp pains that darted throughout my right one. Somehow I was able to get on my feet. Each time I put any pressure on my right leg I would want to scream and topple over. I hopped into the police man's arms and cried to him.

I don't know why I felt like I needed to ask him, "Why would he do this?" The police officer said, "It was just a stupid kid who got inspired." I didn't quite understand what he meant by 'inspired,' but I let it go.

As he helped me reach the hole in the wall, I spotted my pink iPhone charger case overturned in the bloody water. I remembered that Angela's phone was inside of there so I bent down, and picked it up. I clinched it in my hands and told myself not to drop it. I told myself that I would give it back to her once this was all over. I truly believed that I was going to be able to.

I was near the hole, I could see lights and a ton of police officers on the other side. I had let go of the police officer. How I was going to get through the hole in the wall? I thought.

I looked back at him and said "I can't lift my legs," he said "Then sit on your butt, and fall out," I turned around and sat on my bottom, then suddenly I felt someone place their arms underneath my armpits, and pull me on the grass. I screamed in agony as the person ran, with their hands wrapped around my wrists. I saw a ton of people watching me being pulled by my arms, as my legs dangled like bloody rag dolls, bouncing over every small mound. I never stopped screaming. Even when we reached the pickup truck I kept screaming. I was in an unbearable amount of pain. They lifted me onto the back and rushed me to the ambulance. I remember looking at people hovered over top of me telling me to hang in there. I remember looking up past their heads at the palm trees, and the indigo blue sky. I was in a trance, a trance of shock, pain, and heartache. I just stopped screaming…I just stared at everything flying around me for a moment. I was just there — floating.

Once we reached the ambulance I had to get moved onto the stretcher. I shook my head frantically at the EMTs, because I knew what level of pain I was about to be in if they moved me. But it had to happen, whether I wanted it to or not. In a quick 1, 2, 3 they lifted me up and placed me gently on the bed. Of course, I screamed, no matter how fast or how softly they put me down it felt like my leg was ripping away from my body. I remember looking at my legs, the door of the ambulance, and the bottom of the stretcher as they lifted me inside. That picture is stuck in my head, the image of my legs against the backdrop of that closed ambulance door.

They started to cut my clothes off. I groaned over each bump the truck flew over.

"Can you try to ease up on the bumps!" the EMT yelled to the driver.

I was just trying my best to refrain from getting hysterical. I felt myself just wanting to lose it in the back of that ambulance. But they kept telling me that I was going to be okay and asking me questions about myself. After they cut my shorts off, they uncovered another gunshot wound in my left leg. That was a shock to me — I had no idea that I was shot twice. The pain I felt in my right took all the attention away from the left.

When we arrived at the hospital, they transported me to a room, where there were about 6 or 7 different doctors and nurses. It was such a blur, but I remember them telling me that they needed to get some information from me.

"What's your name? How old are you? Where's your family?" they asked.

The questions kept coming, and so did they medics. I was still scared, even though I wasn't inside pulse anymore I was still fearful that the snipers the shooter mentioned would try to blow up the nearby hospitals. I didn't tell the doctors, and nurses that, I just waited to see what the rest of the day would bring.

I was about to speak to my father, I was calm, the nurse handed me the phone after dialing the 10 digit number I told her. I memorized my father's number just in case I ever lost my phone. Today I was glad I did.

"Dad," I called to him.

"Yes," he said in a very confused tone.

It was early in the morning, I've never called that early before.

"I've been shot... I'm in Orlando," I said extremely calm and clear. I didn't want my father to hear the fear in my voice, I didn't want him to feel the pain in my legs, or the sense the death I just witnessed.

"What!?" he yelled.

"I'm ok, I'm ok, I was shot in my legs, but Dad I'm going to be okay," I told him. I was weak, and I couldn't handle explaining all the details to my father at that moment. That's what he needed, that's what he deserved as a parent — details. But I just couldn't give him that.

"Dad, Dad," I tried to stop him from going off on a tangent.

"Dad the lady is going to speak to you now. I'm about to go into surgery," I handed the phone back to the nurse.

I heard her talking to my father for a few more minutes. I know my father was scared, because he didn't know what was going on, and I know he was angry that he couldn't be there to protect me. Nevertheless, I couldn't keep talking to him on the phone. I just needed to be silent, and stare at the medics all around me. I needed to hear the noise, and drown myself in it. I was still waiting to see if death would reappear in the form of an explosion at the hospital, or more machine guns down the halls. I just wanted to wait.

A doctor came in and explained that I would have to be transported to a different hospital for surgery because they didn't have the resources to perform the type of surgery I needed. I still didn't know what that was yet. I didn't bother to ask, I knew the bullet invaded my temple and did something bad, and really, that's all I needed to know. Before I knew it, my bed was moving through the hallways, through an elevator, then through two double doors. I was being pushed into a big room with a light in the middle of the floor like all those ER shows have when they're about to operate. I was quiet, it was nothing else to say, nothing else to cry about, I was here. They put the mask over my face, and then everything went black.

Lesson #3: Some things can never be explained.

5

Survivor's Guilt

When I woke up after surgery Ms. Nicole, Mr. Arthur, and Amir were just walking in. For some strange reason, Amir and I locked eyes. It was a quick but extremely long look at the same time. It was like his soul whispered to me something to me that I couldn't fully understand. I gazed into his eyes trying to figure it out. I only met him once before, but I felt like I was looking at him for the first time.

"Hey, how you feeling?" Ms. Nicole asked.

"I'm in a lot of pain," I said.

"Yeah, I know getting shot ain't no joke," Mr. Arthur replied.

"Did you guys find Angela?" I asked.

"No, we've been to hospital after hospital and no one knows where she is," Ms. Nicole said.

"Yeah. This is the last one," Mr. Arthur added.

Their words settled deep into my heart. Having no information was just like having bad news.

"What about Tanya?" I asked wishing for a better response.

"She's okay, they have her in the hospital next door," Ms. Nicole said.

"Oh ok," I replied.

She called Ms. Claire's phone so I could speak to her. Once she handed me the phone I only exchanged a few words before getting hysterical. I don't remember what Ms. Claire said to me. I just started crying extremely hard. I cried so hard that Ms. Nicole took her phone from me and left the room. I don't remember much after that, I must've fallen back to sleep.

When I woke up I couldn't stop watching the news. A nurse came in to give me more pain medicine.

"Maybe you should take a break from watching the news," she said.

"I know," I replied.

I just couldn't turn it off. I needed to make sure that it was all real. My pain was real, yet my brain struggled with processing what happened. Everything went from good to bad so quickly. Watching the news was my way of getting confirmation. A confirmation that the world was as ugly as I feared growing up. I was glued to the news. I remember watching the death toll rise higher and higher. The names of deceased victims kept scrolling endlessly at the bottom of the screen. I was in complete shock. I was shocked that I was there and shocked that I survived.

I stared at the clear plastic bag that my doctors brought me earlier. It was underneath the table on the floor. It contained my belongings from the night of the shooting. Everything in it was covered in blood. I lost my phone at the club, but I had Angela's. I also had her ID, credit cards, and money that I held for her.

It was so surreal. I was stuck in a daze filled with confusion and agony unable to pull myself out. Tanya was discharged from the hospital the next day. Ms. Claire was bringing her over to see me. I couldn't wait to look at her. I knew to see her face, her bandages, and her pain would mean accepting reality. As I waited for their arrival, I began to feel extremely lonely. There were so many people coming in and out of my room, and I still felt completely alone.

I tried calling my dad over and over again but his phone was off. Not being able to reach him broke my heart. I knew his phone couldn't have been turned off intentionally. He probably wasn't able to pay the bill since he just started his new job. Thankfully, my oldest brother Mick reached out through the hospital phone that same day.

"Hey sis, how you feeling?" he said.

"I'm in a lot of pain, but I'm doing okay," I replied.

"Okay, well I just wanted to let you know that I'm driving down to see you," he said.

"Oh wow thank you, bro, I can't wait until you get here," I said.

"Of course, of course. I know you down there by yourself and I can't even imagine," he said.

"Yeah," I replied.

"Well, you get some rest because I'm going to be there," he said.

"Okay, bro," I replied.

I felt him smile through the phone and say, "Love you, sis."

"Love you too, bro," I smiled back.

I couldn't wait to see him. Mick came into my life once I went off to college. He messaged me through Facebook saying that he wanted to make up for the lost time. I was so happy he came back into my life. He wasn't just there when I needed him for money. He was also there for late night phone calls when I felt like giving up on school. And sure enough, he was there for me again. I'll never forget that.

* * *

I had to use a bedpan for the first time in my life. I remembered senior citizens using them in movies, but I never thought that I'd be using one at 20 years old. Recovering from the shooting was more painful than being shot. I was in shambles physically and mentally. The emotional pain always hurt worse.

I couldn't wash or sit up in bed without assistance. Standing on my feet was complete torture. The pressure surrounding my wounds made me want to fall over. All that "helplessness" was new to me. I was used to standing strong and independently. The whole idea of relying on others was hard to fathom. I was broken and scarred from something I couldn't even explain. My soul cried out for a new body. I felt completely hopeless. Although, I was extremely grateful to be alive, I was extremely bitter about my physical condition. At times I became infuriated thinking about the shooter. I wanted to hurt him as he hurt me.

I just want to get up and go, I thought.

Unfortunately, I couldn't because I was completely immobilized. It felt like God clipped my wings, I couldn't soar anymore. I hated every second of recovery.

My surgeon and a few other doctors entered my room. I had to stop sulking for a moment. They explained the procedures performed during my surgery. There were so many big medical terms flying around, but all I heard was 'shattered,' 'metal rod' and 'bullet fragment.' The bullet that entered my right thigh shattered part of my femur. They showed me an X-Ray of what my femur looked like before the surgery, and my jaw dropped to the floor. I knew I was in a lot of pain, but wow. I had no idea that a single bullet could shatter bone into tiny pieces. My femur looked like a broken Christmas ornament.

They showed me another X-Ray of what my femur looked like after the surgery, and I was amazed. There was a long metal rod going down my thigh. It was connected to screws drilled in at the top and bottom. I felt like a science experiment.

"When the swelling goes down you'll be able to start physical therapy," my surgeon said before leaving my room.

Physical therapy? I thought.

Hearing those words sent chills down my spine. I was in pain while lying completely still. The thought of actually moving my leg was terrifying. I was not looking forward to physical therapy. I never dealt with an injury of that magnitude before. Ironically, I had never been shot before, although, I'm from Philadelphia nicknamed 'Kila-Delphia' for its gun violence. And, on top of that, I never broke any bones before. Now, I was dealing with being shot and broken bones at that same. I never felt so victimized before.

"Why?" I asked God.

"Why did this have to happen to me?" I continued.

"Why did this have to happen to anyone?" I added.

I just laid in my bed sulking, absorbing the news, and watching people come in and out. There was so much going on. So many people going in and out of my room. Nice people, happy people, understanding people...just tons of people. Chaplains, nurses, FBI agents, and the list goes on. I was on so much morphine that they were all a blur. Except for Ms. Sharon, she led the patient experience team at Florida Hospital Orlando, and was also the sweetest lady in the entire world.

She entered my room and said, "Hi Patience, I heard about your story and wanted to pray for you, is that okay?"

"Yeah that's fine, thank you," I replied.

She grabbed my hand and took a deep breath before praying. I could feel how much she truly cared just by the way she grasped my hand. Her prayer was extremely beautiful. Her soft voice filled my room and uplifted my spirits. Although, it was weird having a stranger pray over me I was grateful she was there.

"You're going to be okay Ms. Patience," she said.

"Thank you," I smiled.

"If there's anything you need me to do just let me know, Okay?" she said.

Suddenly, I remembered that Angela was still missing.

"Can you help me find someone?" I asked.

"Yeah sure, um, just give me their name and I'll pass the information on to the right people," she said.

She looked around the table for a notepad then found one.

"Okay, spell their name for me," she said.

I spelled it aloud for her.

She wrote it down neatly and said, "Okay, I got it."

"What does she look like?" she asked.

I remembered Angela's ID was still in the bag on the floor.

"I have her ID, it's in that clear bag right there," I said pointing at the floor.

Ms. Sharon picked up the bag and stared at it.

"You should probably use gloves," I suggested.

"You're right," she said.

She slid on a pair of rubber gloves and opened the bag. A terrible stench filled the room. My clothes were damped and reeked of blood. She laid everything out on the table. I had one sandal on when they rescued me. There was only one in the bag. My purse was brown, it used to be beige. It held the gum I bought from 7-Eleven, my passport, money and Angela's belongings. After sifting through my purse she pulled out her ID. I hoped that would be enough to find her.

* * *

My phone was ringing off the hook. There were so many reporters trying to speak with me. I wasn't sure how they found out my information. One producer called from CNN asking me to share my story live on air. They just wanted to understand what happened, and so did the rest of the world.

I watched the news and realized that my experience was a lot different from other survivors that were speaking out. News stations were trying to figure out the motive behind the shooter's actions. I was in the bathroom with him for three hours and heard him speak. I heard him say what his motive was. I felt obligated to tell my story. The truth was important for me to share.

I agreed to speak with CNN. They put me on live air from my hospital phone. I told them everything from start to finish. I didn't spare any details.

Later that day, my hospital's public relations team came into my room. After my interview with CNN, there were reporters coming to the hospital. They wanted to ask me questions.

"Instead of doing a bunch of interviews, we put together a press conference," a PR agent said.

"Okay," I agreed.

I thought that was the best thing to do. They scheduled the press conference for the following day. Other survivors were going to be present as well. That made me feel a lot better. I never did a press conference before so I was a little nervous. I just wanted to get my story out. And, I was also curious to see what other survivors had to say.

"Also, Jetblue is providing free flights for family members," another PR agent said.

"So, if you have any family that's coming to see you let them know right away," they added.

I called my brother back immediately. Luckily, I caught him before he got on the road. I told him all he had to do was contact JetBlue. The word got out about the free flights to Orlando pretty quickly. Family members who weren't exactly close to me called asking me about them. My own sister...Kate called me and asked about them. I hadn't spoken to her in months.

"Hello," I answered hesitantly.

"Hey sis!" she shouted enthusiastically.

Her voice was so recognizable I knew it was her right away.

"Hey, Kate!" I shouted back.

I adored my sister Kate. We didn't see each other much, but when we did it was amazing. I was so happy to hear her voice, and I could just picture her bright bubbly smile in my head as she spoke.

"Sis, you know it's my birthday this weekend right?" she said.

Birthday weekend? Wait, pause, I thought.

"I heard they were giving out them free flights to Orlando…" she continued.

"Yeah…" I said in disbelief.

I knew where the conversation was headed, and I almost didn't want her to finish.

"I wanted to bring my girl down with me," she said

"Oh ok," I replied.

"Maybe you could talk to someone about getting me and her some tickets or something?" she asked.

I couldn't believe her. I loved my sister dearly, but I almost died. Her little sister was just shot and could've been killed. She should've asked about my wellbeing first. The flights were for family members who wanted to be there to support their loved ones. Not for people that just wanted a free trip to Orlando for their birthday. She didn't even say she wanted the free flight to come to see me. I was so hurt I couldn't even get mad.

"Sure," I lied.

"Okay, thanks, sis! But how are you doing though? You ok?" she asked.

"I'm doing okay," I said calmly.

"Okay good, good," she said.

"So maybe I should give you my information, or you going to have somebody reach out or…" she continued.

"Yeah, I'll just have somebody reach out to you from the hospital," I lied again.

"Okay cool, sis. I'm going to holler at you later then," she said.

"Bye," I said.

After the call with my sister, I looked at everyone that asked about the free flights differently. I couldn't decipher between the people who actually cared about seeing me and the people who just wanted a free vacation. It was several family members who called, including my crazy aunt Linda. Given our history, I couldn't understand why she would even think I'd want to see her. I didn't want to see anyone except for Mick. He was the only one willing to drive from South Carolina. Just to see me, his little sister who almost lost her life. If there was anyone in my family that I wanted to see, it was him. Not even my own dad, who I still wasn't able to get in contact with. I became extremely bitter.

* * *

A lot happened in two days. The days felt extremely long. I was only in the hospital for a couple of them, but it felt like forever. My nurses and doctors began to feel like family. They were so sweet and understanding. I knew they felt bad for me because I didn't have any family there yet. And I felt bad for them too. I couldn't imagine how emotionally taxing it was to uplift so many broken people at once. They must have been tired.

Tanya was discharged and Ms. Claire brought her over to see me. They

71

came in while I was watching the news. Tanya walked in extremely slow and had a brace on her arm. It kept her from agitating her wound on her side. Ms. Claire sat at the bottom of my bed. Tanya hugged me gently then sat in the chair next to my bed. I was happy to see her. Looking at her made everything more real.

"I wasn't going to rest until I knew where you and Angela were at," she said with tears in her eyes.

"Yeah, the doctors had to give her medicine to calm her butt down," Ms. Claire said.

"Oh wow," I replied.

"Did you guys hear anything about Angela?" I asked.

Suddenly, they stopped talking.

Neither of them answered me. Tanya turned her head away from me, and then Ms. Claire did too. I just kept breathing in and out very slowly. My room got so quiet I could hear how quickly my heartbeat sped up. I patiently waited for a response. I didn't move or blink. The silence started to make me nervous. I just stared at them back and forth, afraid to say another word. Then, Ms. Claire slowly turned her head around and looked at me with tears in her eyes. She placed her hand by my right thigh.

"Angela didn't make it," she said.

It seemed like her words echoed around my entire room. A ton of bricks fell on my shoulders. I couldn't breathe without my eyes watering.

"What?!" I replied sharply.

To say I was in shock would be an understatement. I was completely lost. I couldn't understand why she didn't make it. Before I reached the policeman someone told me that she was breathing and had a pulse.

When I picked up her phone and passed off her ID to Ms. Sharon I didn't think that death was even a possibility. I thought she may have been unconscious in a hospital unable to identify herself, but not dead.

"What do you mean she didn't make it?!" I screamed.

Ms. Claire came to my bedside and consoled me.

"What do you mean she didn't make it?!" I cried.

Ms. Claire kept holding me. I pictured Angela in my head. I remembered looking up at her when we made it outside. I remembered her hair, her face, the indigo night sky that hovered above her head. I remembered her bravery as she ran back inside to be with her cousin. I couldn't understand why she didn't make it. I couldn't understand why she was the only one not here. How could an 18-year-old basketball star, scholar, role model and hero be swept away by the harsh winds of this world? Why not me instead? I kept crying and screaming. I never encountered a death this close before. We danced, laughed, and enjoyed life together for the first time. Which suddenly, became the last time. Suddenly, it was all gone. Suddenly, she was gone.

I took the news about Angela really hard. I became extremely depressed. I'd get caught staring off into space or getting stuck gazing into someone's eyes. Hoping that they could take the sadness away. I felt a mixture of feelings. Guilt was the most prevalent. Sadness and confusion followed. Then, a strong hint of hopelessness glued all my emotions together. It was the perfect mixture for suicidal thoughts, self-pity, and a frown that never left. I didn't know how to deal with loss. My first experience was back in 2007 when my grandmother passed away from leukemia. But, I was young and didn't fully grasp the situation. My grandmother was the only mother I had. She always seemed so strong that I thought she'd live forever. Then out of nowhere, she became weaker and weaker right before my eyes.

She'd always say, "Give me my flowers while I'm alive, because I can't smell them when I'm dead."

That was a deep statement for an elementary schooler to unravel, but I understood. I started picking flowers on my way home from school every single day. I'd pick off any dead leaves and give them to her in a little bouquet. She thought the gesture was adorable.

"You can't just go into people's yards and pick their flowers," she said.

"Okay, Grandma," I replied.

"I don't need any more flowers you gave me enough," she assured me.

Then, one day, she had a stroke when I was home alone with her. I heard her making weird noises from my room so I checked on her. She had a bucket by her bed and was slouched over it drooling uncontrollably.

"Should I call 911?" I asked nervously.

I came closer to her and realized that she couldn't move the left side of her face.

"No, I'm fine," she said.

Her words were so slurred I barely understood her. She told me the left side of her face was completely numb. My grandma Harriet was a proud woman. She didn't need any help from anyone, even when she did. Somehow, she managed to drive herself to the hospital. For the first few days, she was doing ok. Then suddenly, she wasn't. My grandmother was diagnosed with leukemia back in her 40's. Unfortunately, she didn't tell anyone and refused treatment.

When she went in for the stroke, they treated her for leukemia too. However, the cancer was left untreated so long it was already too late. She was only 62 years old when she died. One of my family members took me to the hospital to see her for the last time. I sat next to her bed and stared at her for several minutes. I secretly hoped was going to wake up, but she didn't. I just held her swollen hand until I was forced to leave. I didn't shed any tears about her passing until a year later. I felt like she prepared me for her death. I had time to process the fact that she was withering away. But, finding out about Angela's death was different. She was murdered. There was no time to process anything. Death just came in and stole her. There was no time to give her flowers. And, any chance I had of building our friendship was ripped away.

Shortly after getting the news about Angela, her family was on their way to visit me. I even couldn't bear the thought of looking at her mother and father in the face. I just knew they must've been heartbroken, upset, and angry about Angela being robbed from them. I started crying just thinking about the pain they must've felt.

"They're strong people," Ms. Claire said.

"But, you have to try and hold it together for them," she continued.

I didn't exactly know how to do that. Angela's family started walking in. This time Amir brought his infant daughter, and the mother of his child, Haile. I was surprised to see her because Tanya told me they weren't together anymore. Amir came over to me and gave me a big hug. I needed it, plus he smelled really nice. I didn't mind Haile being there, but she didn't speak to me at all. I thought it was weird since she was in my hospital room. The least you could do is say hello to the person hospitalized. It was no big deal, just very weird. Needless to say, I had a full room. My nurse, Ms. Jackie, a strong woman with an even stronger Caribbean accent, felt like it was too many people in my room at once. She was afraid of the commotion being too much for me.

"If you want some people to leave just let me know, I'll throw them out," she whispered.

Maybe she sensed the weird energy in the room too.

"It's okay, I'm alright," I said.

"Okay, but if you need me just call me in," she said.

My facial expressions must've shown how I really felt. Honestly, it was too much for me. I just wanted to be alone. I wanted to cry and scream all by myself. Nevertheless, I couldn't do that with them there. So, I held it in for as long as I could. After we watched a vigil that the city of Philadelphia put together for Angela I just couldn't hold it in anymore. When it was time for me to use my bedpan I asked my nurse to kick everyone out. Ms. Claire refused to leave.

"You don't have to feel embarrassed around me," she said.

"I know Ms. Claire," I replied.

When I was finished Ms. Nicole was the first person to reenter the room. I was glad because I wanted to speak to her. I needed a moment to express all of my feelings to her. I wanted to give her an opportunity to respond. I wanted her to lay it all on me, and be honest about how she felt.

"Ms. Nicole," I called.

"Yes, baby?" she replied.

Before I could form any sentences I started crying. I told her how sorry I was for everything that happened. I let her know how responsible I felt for being outside with Angela, then suggesting we go back in together.

"I should have just told her to stay outside while I went in alone," I cried.

"You shouldn't blame yourself," she said.

"Anyone of you would have gone back in for the other one," she continued.

"Y'all came together and y'all were supposed to leave together," she added.

Her words surprised me and gave me a huge sense of relief. I thought she was going to hate me, but she didn't. So, at that moment, I made the decision to stop hating myself. Hearing her say those words helped me let go of some survivor's guilt.

Lesson #4: Don't blame yourself for things you can't control.

There's a great deal of pain that comes with surviving.
  You smile, say "I'm okay,"
  Even when your soul feels like dying.

You keep trying,
  But you can't erase what you saw,
  You can't escape those walls,
  Your wounds too raw,
  I know, I've been there.

But you can't give up,
  Even when rising is too much,
  You have to find a way
  to corrupt those intruding memories,
  and let your healing begin.

Find your strength within,
  cheesy I know, but TAP IN.

And when you're tapped out,
  Lean on your support,
  ask for help then ask for more,
  and keep asking until you feel better,
  Write in your journal,
  Read open letters,
  Share your pain, open up,
  Because bottling just isn't enough.

You're a warrior, you're tough.
  But it's okay to ask for help when you need it,
  Don't stuff everything inside,
  Trauma becomes a monster when you feed it.
  Defeat it.

6

The Journal and I

I couldn't sleep when everyone left. People kept making noises in the hall that scared me. I wanted to close my door to limit the noise, but I couldn't. I felt trapped when the door was closed. I needed to leave my door open. I felt safer when the door was open for some reason. I just stayed up watching the news. Nurse Jackie was on duty for the night. She came in to give me my medicine and saw that I wasn't planning on going to sleep anytime soon. She handed me a small pink journal, with a tiny floral pen attached to its side. She told me to write.

"Just take everything you're feeling inside and put it on paper," she said.

"I'll try," I replied.

I wasn't in a writing mood. If I tried to write something right away it wouldn't be genuine. That's not the type of writer I am. I had to feel it first. I needed a moment to sit in the silence and listen to my emotions cry out. I needed to hear my own whimpers, and sighs of sadness to know when and where to begin. I stared at the journal for a while. I didn't touch it or move it. I just stared at it, while listening to the news play in the background. Then suddenly, I got the urge to pick it up.

Just try to write something, I thought.

I didn't know what I was going to say. But, whenever I felt compelled to write I'd jot the first thing down that came to mind. I never knew what the outcome was going to be, nevertheless, it always came out beautiful. Creative writing was always a way for me to cope with pain. Especially when I felt like my pain was being silenced. Unfortunately, this pain was extremely different. It was really difficult for me to grapple with. This pain was foreign and came with a lot of layers. I had so many emotions clouding my mind and spirit. I couldn't just pick one place to stem my writing from.

I'd feel bitter and angry about being injured. I just wanted to walk again. Then, I'd feel extremely ungrateful about being angry. I felt like I didn't deserve the right to be angry about my injury, because it was victims, like Angela, who weren't even alive to feel the pain that I was feeling. So, I'd feel lucky to be alive. However, when I felt luckier, I felt guiltier. I survived, but so many others did not. The words started coming to me out of nowhere.

"The guilt of being alive is heavy…." I wrote.

"Wanting to smile about surviving, but not sure if the people around you are ready…" I continued.

I crossed out sentences, ripped a few pages, and started completely over before I put my pen down. It was a process, but when I was done, I felt like a weight had been lifted off my shoulders. I could breathe deep again. I could even sleep again. All of my emotional pain was in that little pink journal. I didn't have to carry it inside of me anymore.

* * *

It was the day of the press conference and Mick wasn't able to make it. His flight had a ton of stops, which made a three-hour flight turn into an eight-hour flight. Ms. Claire thought that Mick would be there, so she left to check on Tanya. He wasn't scheduled to land until later that night. I didn't want to bother Ms. Claire by asking her to come back. Besides, Tanya needed her too. Ms. Claire was her mom, not mine.

I had a few visitors from Fox 29 News before the press conference started. Kile, a videographer, and Curt, a reporter were covering the story for everyone back at home. But they didn't come to my room to interview me. They came to see how I was doing. It was so strange to me. I remembered learning from them while I was interning at Fox 29 News. Now, they were in my hospital room in Orlando, FL.

"Everyone back at home is really worried about you," Curt said.

"Yeah, we just wanted to make sure you were alright," Kile added.

"Thank you so much, that means a lot to me," I replied.

They let me know that everyone back at the station was praying for me. That really touched my heart. I wasn't sure if any of them really remembered my name half the time. But, hearing about how worried they were showed me that they did notice me. They couldn't stay for too long, because I had to get ready to go downstairs. Curt was headed back to Philadelphia, but Kile was staying to cover the press conference.

"See you downstairs," Kile said.

"See ya," I replied.

Shortly after they left, the hospital's public relations team came in. They let me know the logistics of the press conference.

"All of the survivors will be given the opportunity to say what they want before any questions are asked," a PR agent said.

"Okay," I replied.

"The press will be given an opportunity to ask questions after you've shared your story," another PR agent added.

"Ok, that's fine," I replied.

I didn't say too much to them, because I was nervous. Even though they told me what would happen, but I didn't know what to expect in actuality. I pictured a ton of reporters with notepads shoving microphones in my face. That's how I recalled the press conferences on the TV shows I watched.

It was time for me to move. My nurses said they weren't able to take me downstairs in my bed. They asked me to use the wheelchair instead and parked it by my bed. I didn't want to move at all. I wore an immobilizer to keep my leg straight at all times. My nurses helped me reach the wheelchair. But, unfortunately, the wheelchair wasn't compatible with my immobilizer. It had a sturdy leg extender, but it was too low. When I tried to sit down it wasn't high enough to keep my leg from bending...so it bent.

"Omg. I can't do it, I can't do it," I cried.

"Okay okay, we'll figure something else out," a nurse said.

My leg didn't bend much, but it was enough to agitate the entire surgery area. The pain grew quickly and became unmanageable. The only solution was for me to sit in my recliner with the leg rest extended. Sometimes, I would sit next to the window and admire the city's beauty.

I imagined what our vacation would've been like without the shooting. Luckily, the recliner had wheels at the bottom. My nurses gave me pain medicine before heading downstairs. I was already nervous about speaking, and extremely emotional. But now, I was drowsy. I wasn't sure how I was going to make it through my entire story without passing out. I didn't even know where to begin. There was so much to tell from one night.

Read your poem, I thought.

I decided to bring my journal down with me. The poem was an easier way for me to communicate my story to the public. It was words on a piece of paper that truly embodied all of my emotions. However, I didn't plan on reading the poem right away, it just was there for safety.

I finally reached the conference room. There was only one other survivor there. His name was Larry. He was lying on his stretcher with his family standing beside him. He was shot multiple times his body and foot. I didn't remember seeing him at the club, but he said he remembered seeing me.

"Where are you from?" I asked.

"I'm from Philadelphia," he replied.

"No way, I'm from Philadelphia too," I said.

"Wow, it's such a small world," he replied.

"You ready?" a nurse said to me.

I thought that was a crazy coincidence, but I was too drowsy to continue talking. The pain medicine was already kicking in high gear, and I needed to save my energy.

"Yes," I replied.

They opened the door and wheeled me in first. I heard tons of cameras flashing as soon as the door opened. The room swallowed me whole. They rolled me to a spot in the middle of the floor. The room was full of videographers, photographers, and reporters holding recorders to document anything they possibly could. They wheeled in Larry right after me. Having him there made me feel more comfortable. I stared into the crowd and absorbed the energy. Suddenly, I wasn't nervous anymore. Maybe, it was the pain medicine, or maybe my soul found peace.

Larry began speaking first. He detailed everything that happened from his point of view. It was very different from my experience. He was in another part of the club during the shooting. I was tuned into each word he said. I felt the fear in his voice and realized that we survived something we shouldn't have. When he finished his last sentence he passed the microphone over to me. Reporters began throwing questions at him like darts.

"Where are you from?" a reporter shouted.

"Why were you at Pulse that night?" another journalist yelled.

"Excuse me!" a PR agent interjected.

"You will have an opportunity to ask questions at the end," they continued.

I held the microphone in my hand for a few seconds before speaking, and stared into the hungry eyes of journalists who only wanted the facts. I breathed deep and reflected on the reason why we were all there. I wanted every single person in the room to remember why as well. I pictured Angela's face right before she ran back inside and died in her cousin's arms. I started to feel the pain that I wrote in my journal all over again. I wanted the crowd to understand the pain that I was feeling before they could ask me anything. I wasn't just a part of a story, Angela wasn't just a supporting detail, and the shooting wasn't just an eye-catching headline. This was life, and Angela's life was cut short, my body was damaged and Tanya was traumatized forever. So I decided to read the poem first.

"Before I start to share my story..." I said.

"I want to recite a poem that I wrote in the middle of the night last night, which really shows everything that I'm feeling right now. And it's part of my healing process, writing, so..." I continued.

I took a deep breath and began to read:

The guilt of feeling grateful to be alive is heavy.

Wanting to smile about surviving,

but not sure if the people around you are ready.

As the world mourns the people killed and viciously slain,

I feel guilty about screaming about my legs in pain because I can feel nothing,

like the other 49 who weren't so lucky to feel this pain of mine.

I never thought in a million years this could happen.

I never thought in a million years my eyes could witness something so tragic.

Looking at the souls leaving the bodies of individuals,

looking at the killer's machine gun throughout my right peripheral,

looking at the blood and debris covered on everyone's faces,

looking at the gunman's feet under the stall as he paces.

The guilt of feeling lucky to be alive is heavy.

It's like the weight of the ocean's walls crushing uncontrolled by levees.

It's like being drug through the grass with a shattered leg and thrown on the back of a Chevy,

and being rushed to the hospital and told you're going to make it,

when you laid beside individuals whose lives were brutally taken.

The guilt of being alive is heavy.

After I read my poem I felt like everyone in the room was on the same page with me. I was ready to share my full story. I detailed everything that happened from beginning to end. I didn't spare any details. I even mentioned the money print boots, hair bangs, and glasses that Emily wore that night. I wanted to paint a vivid picture for everyone. I wanted the journalists to walk visually with me, and imagine everything that I described.

I took my time, I didn't rush through my story. I wanted them to picture the three of us dancing, laughing, and having a blast. Then, I wanted them to picture our entire lives being disrupted forever. I wanted them to feel my truth, not just report it. Despite how emotional I was, I didn't cry the entire time I spoke.

When I finished, the reporters began asking questions right away. I answered a few without a problem. But, I kept picturing Angela's face in my head, Tanya holding her side, and people dying all around me. I kept reflecting on why we were all there, over and over again. And, the more I kept reflecting, the less I wanted to be there answering questions.

"What do you do for a living?" a reporter shouted.

What do I do for a living? I thought.

The question seemed inappropriate to me at that time. I didn't think my occupation had anything to do with my story. My occupation wasn't going to bring Angela back, or make the shooting go away. I thought the question was irrelevant. I didn't even answer I just started crying. I completely broke down, and couldn't regain composure. Now, I realize the reporter was just doing their job. But, at that time, I was struggling with survivor's guilt. I felt like I didn't deserve to survive because so many others did not. Then, hearing a reporter ask about my profession just made me feel even worse. One of my physicians, Dr. Finner, came over to me.

"Do you want to leave?" he asked.

"Yes," I cried.

"Okay, we're done here," he announced.

"We're going to take her back upstairs," he continued.

Suddenly, the room transformed into a tiny box that I was suffocating in. The strong mask I wore in the beginning melted away, and my true face was left. I was broken, wounded and scared. My nurses took me back to my room. I needed some time alone to decompress.

My entire hospital staff said they were extremely proud of me. But I didn't think that I did anything to deserve recognition. I told my story the best way I knew how. But, to my surprise, when I turned on the TV every news channel was replaying a clip of my poem. I was completely shocked. It was so strange to see myself on the screen. I thought I looked like hell. I could see the pain all over my face, and it made me emotional. When I watched clips of me breaking down, I wanted to cry all over again. I hated seeing myself so weak when I wanted to be strong.

* * *

Later that same day, I met Ms. Karlie, she was a key executive at Florida Hospital Orlando. Her positive energy filled the room the moment she walked in. She introduced herself, then explained how much my poem touched her heart. I felt honored to have someone like her support me. She was definitely a boss lady. Her hair was perfect, and her make up was flawless. Not to mention, the stylish business suit she wore. But, above all, she seemed very sincere. It felt like she genuinely wanted to be there for me.

"If there's anything you need at all, just let me know," she said.

All of a sudden, I thought about my hair. My scalp was super itchy, and the extensions I had installed for a vacation looked awful. Remnants of the mass shooting lived in my hair. Whenever I scratched my head sprinkles of debris fell on my face. Cement dust and tiny pieces of sheetrock lingered on my scalp from the police busting through the club wall. My hair smelled like dried blood, and toilet water. I explained all of this to her the best I could.

"I just need a scarf," I said.

"Ok, I'll see what they have downstairs," she replied.

She gave me a big hug before leaving the room. I was happy that I met her. Ms. Karlie wasn't the only person that came to see me that day.

"Patience, you have a visitor," my nurse said.

"Who is it?" I asked.

"It's a local pastor from the community," she replied.

"He just wanted to speak with you, only if you want to," she continued.

"Sure that's fine," I replied.

"Are you sure?" she asked.

"Yeah, I'm sure," I said.

I didn't know anyone in Florida, so I was surprised to have a visitor from the community. The pastor walked in and quickly introduced himself before explaining why he was there.

"I was on my way to work when I heard your poem on the radio," he said.

"I needed to come see you, and share what God placed on my heart," he continued.

"Wow, thank you for coming all the way here," I replied.

"It was no problem at all. Patience, you have a special gift," he said.

"You have a calling with your writing, and I hope you walk in it," he continued.

He seemed really serious. I didn't know what else to say besides thank you. He went out of his way just to share that with me. I always knew I loved to write, but I didn't think it was my calling in life. I told him how much I appreciated his visit and asked him to pray for me. He agreed without hesitation. He held my hand and said a powerful prayer about healing and destiny. It was a short visit, but his words stayed with me for the rest of the day. I was grateful that he came to enlighten me.

I had a few more visitors that day. Different staff members from my hospital stopped by. Most of them just came to hug me. It seemed like every staff member at Florida Hospital was super compassionate. Their level of kindness was inspiring. I also had a visit from an NYU director. He led an NYU chapter in south Florida. I didn't even know that existed, but I was glad to find out. His visit made feel extremely appreciated by my school community.

Then I had a couple of visits from the FBI. First, a male agent showed up and asked me to share my story with him. I repeated everything I said in the press conference. He left quickly after that. Then, two female agents dropped by. They didn't really say too much. But, they asked if they could see my poem. I handed them my journal with no hesitation.

"Do you mind if we take a picture?" one of them asked.

"Sure," I said curiously.

She took one quick photo on her iPhone. Then they said goodbye and left. I wasn't sure why they needed the picture. I didn't bother to ask why they were the FBI.

The hospital gave me a tablet to communicate with my family and friends. My cellphone was left at the club, and I wasn't able to get it back. When I logged into my Facebook I had over a thousand notifications. There was so much love and support coming my way. My family members, people I knew from grade school, interns I worked with at FOX 29 News, and even strangers were sending me uplifting messages. Media outlets from all around the world shared a clip of my poem. I couldn't believe the incredible response I received from one moment of vulnerability.

Maybe writing is my calling, I thought.

* * *

It was time for me to start physical therapy. I dreaded the thought of it, but there was nothing I could do. It was the only way for me to get better. I had to force myself to push through. It definitely wasn't a stroll on the beach. My physical therapist told me that I'd walk again. I was extremely relieved to hear that. Nevertheless, I thought about the kind of walk I would have. I asked him if I was going to have a permanent limp. I knew my scars weren't going anywhere, but a limp wasn't something I could put makeup on.

"As long as you do your best in physical therapy, you should be fine," he said.

That answer wasn't good enough for me. There was a slight possibility that I could have a permanent limp for the rest of my life. Just thinking about those odds infuriated me. I couldn't believe the shooter destroyed my precious body. I wanted revenge, but I knew that I couldn't have it. And knowing that made me more upset.

I tried my best to let everything go. I tried my best to focus on healing. Unfortunately, I had several emotional breakdowns before I could start my first PT session. I admit self-pity and anger got the best of me. I didn't want to look at the bright side of things. I didn't want to hear about how long it would take to recover. I didn't want to have to recover from anything at all.

After I finally came to my senses, my nurse began transporting me to the PT room down the hall. A few hospital staff stopped to give me a hug along the way. But, one nurse hugged me longer than everyone else. I held onto her because I assumed she felt strongly about the shooting. I thought she probably felt sorry for me and got really emotional. All of a sudden, she started crying in my arms. I felt her entire body trembling. I didn't know what to do besides hold her. My nurse rubbed her back and helped me console her. I just kept embracing her until she moved back, and stared into my eyes. I could see the pain in hers.

"You were with my niece, Emily," she said.

"Omg…" I replied.

Her words hit me like a ton of bricks. I didn't know what to say. I started to see the resemblance between them.

"When you were describing the girl with the glasses, and the bang I knew you were talking about my Emily," she cried.

"She didn't make it," she continued.

I couldn't believe it. It felt like someone gripped my lungs in their palms and squeezed them. I kept staring at her, trying to remember how to breathe properly. I held her hand and cried with her.

"I'm so sorry, she was so sweet," I said.

I wondered how she felt looking at me. I spent the last few moments with someone she loved so dearly. I didn't know how to feel. Emily brought joy to my life within the first 60 seconds of meeting her. She was extremely kind, warm, and bubbly. I could only imagine the joy she brought to her family.

After my PT session, Emily's aunt came to my room. She handed me a brown journal that had a tree engraved on the cover. There was a scripture on the front, and it said Blessed is the man who trusts in the Lord.

"Thank you so much," I said.

"No problem, just keep writing," she replied.

She smiled and said, "You definitely have a gift."

Lesson #5: Find healthy ways to express your pain.

7

Conspiracy

S o much happened in one day. Mick finally showed up, my father called me, and my other siblings reached out. My father told me his cellphone was shut off because he didn't pay the bill. I couldn't stay mad at him for that. I learned to let certain things go when it came to him. My dad suffered enough from his own demons.

My other siblings weren't able to fly down, because of work and their kids. I completely understood that too and didn't hold it against them. Besides, I was extremely happy that Mick was there. Tanya's family members were there for support, but they wanted to give Mick and I time alone. I wanted to give them some time alone as well. They were still processing Angela's death. Although they were really strong people, I knew they had to be crumbling inside.

Luckily, Mick didn't have to sleep on the couch in my room. The hospital sponsored suites for family members at a hotel across the street. I thought that was so amazing. The Orlando community extended so much love and support to me. Care packages and kind letters kept pouring in. Ms. Karlie was able to find a scarf. I took my extensions out immediately. I was so glad she came through for me. My hospital staff gave me whatever I needed to be comfortable. And, they treated my brother the same. They started to feel like family.

My father finally showed up. He did a spectacular job of hiding his feelings. When he saw me in the hospital bed I knew he wanted to cry. Instead, he acted normal by asking if I drank enough water, and scooped crust out the corners of my eyes. His usual routine.

I have to admit that having Mick and my dad in the same room felt a little awkward. They didn't have a great relationship. In fact, they didn't have any relationship. But they were cordial and focused on me. I was proud of them both for putting me first.

To my surprise, another sibling of mine showed up, Terrence. I always thought he had the most swag compared to the rest of us. The other day he told me that he couldn't make it, but there he was. I was sitting in my recliner by the window when he walked in.

"Omg," I cried.

"Hey, sis," he replied gleefully.

I was so emotional, I did NOT expect to see him at all.

"I was going to tell you, but he wanted it to be a surprise," Mick said.

"Haha, yeah, I got you good," Terrence said jokingly.

"This means so much to me, thank you for coming," I said.

"Of course, of course, how you feeling though?" he asked.

"I'm doing okay, hanging in there," I said pointing to my leg.

"Oh sis, your going to be just fine," he said.

I hugged him for a really long time. Terrence had a family and work obligations but he figured out a way to get there. I really appreciated him for that. I remembered the time Terrence and his wife Raya came to see me. I lived with my crazy aunt at the time. She was just like my Grandma Harriet, but worse. She didn't let me out of her sight. But, one day she finally let Terrence and Raya take me out. They took me to dinner and even bought me shoes for school. I was so grateful for those shoes because I only had one raggedy pair back then.

"Unfortunately, I have to go back tonight sis," he said regretfully.

"That's fine, I understand, I'm just so happy to see you," I smiled.

Terrence and my father didn't have a great relationship either and I sensed the tension in the room between them. But they remained cordial and focused their energy on me. My brothers had a lot to say to my dad, but they refrained. They needed an explanation for things that happened in the past between him and our mom. But I needed their support more than they needed answers.

* * *

Later that day, I was sitting in my hospital bed watching the news. My brothers were finding food and my dad was "getting some air" (in reality smoking a cigarette). I decided to check my Facebook for new messages. There was a lot. I was never going to sort through them all in one day. I had a bunch of notifications too. Unfortunately, they weren't just from family and friends. They were from conspiracy theorists.

There was a meme circulating that had a screenshot of me behind the Fox 29 News desk in Philadelphia. The words "CRISIS ACTOR" were plastered across the top. The caption said that I was paid by the government to help arrange the "Pulse Shooting Hoax." People were calling me a liar and other derogatory names in the comment section. I was completely crushed and didn't know how to defend myself. I was behind the Fox 29 News desk because I was an intern learning how to read from the teleprompter. I wasn't paid by the government to arrange anything. I was tormented in a bathroom with a mass murderer for three hours. I bled from two gunshots wounds and watched innocent people die inches from me. I couldn't believe that real human beings thought it was fake.

I tried to reply to every single conspiracy theorist. I wrote "You should really be ashamed of yourself," to one of them. It was people who had real families and real jobs that truly believed the conspiracy theorists. I kept commenting and reporting posts. I saw my family members, friends, and strangers lashing back at conspiracy theorists on my behalf. I appreciated everyone who defended me against that nonsense.

It felt like the internet declared war on me. I kept finding new accusations that made me look guilty. But it was all fabricated evidence. One conspiracy theorist took a screenshot of a picture I posted right before I went to Pulse. I worked hard on my make up and was proud of my outfit so I posted a selfie on my social media. However, the person edited the timestamp to falsely prove that I wasn't at Pulse during the shooting. The original timestamp was visible on Twitter, but some people believed the lie anyway. And as the lies continued, more and more claims came out. The memes evolved into full 10-15 minute videos on YouTube. Hate towards Patience Carter

"THE PAID CRISIS ACTOR" was everywhere. I couldn't escape the conspiracy theorists.

Unfortunately, I couldn't escape regular people that just wanted to be negative either. Media outlets continued to post clips of my poem on social media. And the conspiracy theorists found each one as I expected. However, on The Shade Room's Instagram post of me speaking, someone wrote, "how did it turn into a poetry slam though?"Another person said, "Her hair looks a mess," as if I wasn't in the hospital completely immobilized. I was heartbroken, because those comments didn't come from internet trolls hiding behind fake pages. It came from people close to my age, and who went to school just like me. I couldn't understand how people could be so mean during such a difficult time.

It was already bad enough, but my old music video entitled "make a dollar" added fuel to the fire. I saw that a random guy had shared my music video on Facebook, claiming that I was in Orlando to promote my new song when I was shot. That was a complete lie. In addition to that, a news station posted a clip of the music video as well. I didn't give them any permission to do that. I called the station and demanded answers. I was already drowning in conspiracy theories and my old music video didn't help. The station told me that they received permission to play the clip from the producer of the song. But no one ever asked me anything.

When my brothers came back I showed them everything. But they always found a way to make me laugh.

"Aye look, if they talking about you, it must mean you're important," Mick joked.

"Right, someone spending all their time making videos about you, you got to be important," Terrence laughed.

"Yeah let them keep on talking about you!" Mick shouted.

"Yeah, I guess," I said bleakly.

I didn't look at it the way they both did. Although they had a valid point my feelings were still hurt. It was extremely hard to focus on the positive when there was so much negativity being thrown at me.

"Look, sis," Terrence said pulling up a video on his phone.

"What?" I replied.

"Even Hilary Clinton talking about you," he joked.

"What get out of here!" I said sucking my teeth.

"Yeah, look," he replied.

He showed me a video of Hilary Clinton speaking out about the shooting. She mentioned my name, super briefly, but it proved my brothers' point. I didn't think it was a big deal, it wasn't like she followed me on Instagram or anything. But I let him have it.

"Ok, that's crazy," I said.

"Exactly, so people gonna talk about you, good or bad," he joked.

I wanted to care less about what people were saying, but I cared. I kept checking social media every five seconds. I kept responding to conspiracy theorists and exhausting my energy on negativity instead of healing. I had to defend myself in some kind of way. So I started posting on social media — a lot.

I asked my dad to take pictures of me in my hospital bed. I wanted to show them that the shooting wasn't fake. I wanted to let them know that I was really in pain. Nevertheless, they were never satisfied. When I posted the picture my dad took of me, conspiracy theorists ate me alive. They claimed that I was never shot and that the picture was staged. I was so upset that I unstrapped my immobilizer, peeled away from my bandages, and took pictures of my raw wounds. I recorded a few videos as well, just to prove that I wasn't a crisis actor. I hoped it would be enough for them to leave me alone. When I posted the pictures and videos conspiracy theorists claimed that my wounds were fake too. It was an endless battle for my sanity, so I gave up.

It was a long day, and I was extremely tired. Mick returned to his hotel suite. Terrence headed back home and my dad stayed with me. The hospital offered my dad a suite at the hotel, but he didn't want it.

"I'm alright sleeping right here," he said setting up a station on the couch.

He turned on the reading light, put on his glasses, and began flipping through a newspaper. I never asked my dad about how he felt, but I knew that he was tired. I knew there was nothing interesting enough in that newspaper to keep him up all night. I knew he was extremely worried about me. He never shared how scared he was for me, or how terrified he was about what happened. Instead, he read his newspaper all night long. He said nothing, but everything that I needed to hear at the same time. His presence made me feel safe, safe enough to finally sleep with the door closed.

"I love you, dad," I said before dozing off.

"I love you too baby girl, get some rest," he replied.

***

Mick said he wasn't leaving my side until I was discharged. And my dad said he wasn't leaving until the next day. Their presence helped me channel my energy on my recovery, and away from the internet trolls.

Slowly but surely my leg was getting better. I was still in excruciating pain, but I was making progress. The morphine definitely helped me manage. Ms. Claire dropped by a few times to check on me. I appreciated her for sticking by my side. She told me that everyone was doing fine and holding it together.

"If you aren't able to leave by Friday, I'll stay behind with you if your brother can't," she said.

I lowered my head and said, "No, you can't do that."

"Patience, you know I don't mind," she said firmly.

"I wouldn't even feel comfortable with you," I explained.

"Patience, stop it," she said sharply cutting me off.

"If I have to stay, I will," she assured me.

"Okay," I nodded.

I appreciated the gesture, but I didn't want Tanya feeling like her mom was choosing me over her. We went through that issue in the past, and I didn't want to pick any old wounds. I didn't need any "energy shifts" in my life after the shooting. The shooting was a huge energy shift all by itself. On top of that, I didn't want to be a burden to Ms. Claire. She already had a wounded daughter — and her name wasn't Patience. I was determined to make my flight home on Friday.

Later that day, my hospital's PR team came into my room. They were smiling extremely hard, it made me suspicious.

"Heyyy…" I said hesitantly.

"Patience, we have a very important question to ask you," a PR agent replied.

"Okay…." I grinned. I had no idea what to expect.

"Would you like to meet…" she paused.

"The President of the United States?!" she squealed.

"Oh my God, UH-Yeah!" I yelled. I couldn't contain my excitement.

"Okay great! The only thing is, you're only able to bring one guest," she said.

"Oh. Ok. Oh my gosh!" I replied.

I was extremely happy to meet President Barack Obama. Meeting the President of the United States is a big deal for anyone. But meeting the first African-American President of the United States was monumental, iconic, and truly once in a lifetime. He was the symbol of change, and I was going to be in the same room with him. I couldn't believe it.

I was elated, but I dreaded the thought of choosing between Mick and my dad. My dad…was my dad, he had a parental advantage. I felt like I had to choose him, simply because he gave me life. But then again, Mick was the first person to make it to the hospital. And he was willing to drive to Florida just to see me. And he wasn't leaving until I was discharged. It was a hard decision for me to make. I had to talk about it with someone.

Luckily, there were a bunch of nurses that I loved. I can only remember Ms. Jackie, Jodie, and Daria by name. But they were all super nice to me. They treated me like a younger sister. I decided to ask one of them for help. Nurse Daria was around the most during the day, so I talked to her about it. She was already asking me questions about meeting the President anyway.

"Well… Do you know what you're going to say?" she smiled.

"I really don't know haha," I laughed.

"I didn't think I'd ever get the opportunity, so I never really thought about it," I said.

"Aww, it's got to be pretty mind-blowing haha," she joked.

"Yes! Seriously, I have no idea what I'm going to say," I replied.

Then suddenly, I thought about my journal. The brown one Emily's aunt gave me. I called it my book of dreams. I wrote a bunch of magical ideas in there already. I thought about different ways I could inspire someone with my story and jotted them down.

"I'll probably ask him to sign my journal," I said.

"Omg, Patience, that's a great idea! You should definitely ask him to do that! He would totally sign it," she squealed.

"Yeah? Okay cool! I'm going to ask him haha," I giggled.

"Do you know who you're going to pick?" she asked. I didn't even have to bring it up.

"No...not yet, It's just hard, you know?" I said squinting my eyes at her.

"Well...I mean.....Mick was here first, and... hasn't left your side since," she said squinting back at me.

"If you had to choose one, I think it should be Mick," she continued.

"Yeah! You're right," I replied.

I was so glad she said that. My heart wanted to choose Mick anyway, but my mind thought that I should automatically pick my dad, simply because he was my dad. But, Mick truly earned it. Truthfully, he's been earning it since I went off to college. My dad was there for key moments too, but Mick deserved the chance to meet the President. I prayed that my dad would understand my decision.

* * *

I was getting ready to meet the President. Thankfully, Daria reached out to a local celebrity make up artist, Marian Robinson. She asked her to do my make up for my special moment. Marian agreed to do it free of charge. I was so grateful to her. But I immediately thought about Tanya. She hated when I let other MUA's do my make up. Only she could slay my contour and highlight. There was absolutely no way she could have done it. She was healing for goodness' sake, I just wanted her to relax. She was meeting the President too. Although it was for such a terrible reason, I wanted her to focus on being happy about it. We all needed something to be happy about.

I needed my hair done too. Well, I needed hair, because I threw my old extensions out. There was nothing but braids underneath the scarf Ms. Karlie bought me. Daria asked around about a stylist, but luckily, Marian saved the day. She told her friend and philanthropist, Jamie Pappries about my situation. Jamie was so touched by my story, that she donated enough money for me to get a premium 100% human hair wig. If you're not too familiar with the wig world, human hair units are really expensive. Jamie's level of kindness was surreal, and I was extremely grateful for her donation. I didn't have to meet President Obama with hair that smelled like mass murder. Marian brought a stylist to curl the wig for me as well. I appreciated how much she went out of her way to make it all happen. She just met me but embraced me like a daughter.

I was only getting one chance to meet the President. Therefore, I didn't want to look (or smell) like what I'd been through. If I could have gotten out of bed to get myself ready, I would have. But I couldn't, and I wouldn't have been able too for a long time. Before I got dressed Marian and her stylist did their magic. My makeup came out perfect! I didn't want anything too heavy, just a soft natural look. And, Marian nailed it!

When I took my extensions out my nurses helped me brush the debris out of my hair. I put on my new unit and made sure it was secure. Then, my stylist hooked it up. It felt good to feel beautiful again. It felt amazing to be excited about something, even if it was only temporary. I appreciated everyone that helped me get ready. Especially Daria, who went out of her way to buy me an outfit. She brought me a dress, undershirt, shoes, underwear, a necklace, and a bottle of perfume. She didn't have to do any of that, but she did. She was so sweet, I couldn't stop thanking her.

I needed a lot of assistance putting my clothes on. My nurses helped me out so it didn't take too long. However, when it was time to put my underwear on…things got a little awkward. There was no way I could have done it myself, and everyone knew that.

"I'll put them on for you," Daria volunteered.

"Thank you," I replied trying not to laugh.

I was the only one putting my underwear on for a long time. It felt a little weird not being able to do it for myself. But I needed to get more comfortable with depending on people. I couldn't be the stubborn girl I was before. I had to get help and rely on people for things. If I didn't, I was going to suffer in silence, all alone without any clean underwear.

Daria helped me stand up so I could lean on my walker. She got one side of my underwear over my immobilizer. Then, I sat back down and stepped my left foot into the other side. She pulled them up for me, then BOOM! I had on fresh a fresh pair of undies. Daria was the real MVP that day. I'll never forget her.

My PR team asked if a reporter from the Orlando Sentinel could film me getting ready. They wanted to show the public my excitement about meeting President Obama. I didn't think the public was going to care about my excitement, but I said yes anyway. The reporter came in and explained the shots he would need from me.

"Just keep doing what you're doing, pretend I'm not here," he said.

"Okay," I replied doubtfully.

I tried my best to act normal, but it was so strange having a camera in my face. I smiled nervously and glanced at my brother. Mick was so silly that he kept making faces the entire time, and I kept laughing. I was in a happy place, and on a scale from 1 to 10, I was a 10 that day. For a moment I wasn't thinking about the pain or the horror I faced. They made me feel like a princess. I had never felt that way before in my entire life.

Tanya and her mom came over a little later. We were leaving from my hospital to go see the President together. It didn't seem like Tanya was "holding it together" as Ms. Claire said. Her eyes were red as if she had been crying all morning. And it didn't look like she spent any time getting glammed up. I can't imagine what it must've felt like to lose a sister. That's what Angela was like to her, a sister. But I tried my best to stay in a positive mindset for her.

When they walked in, Marian and the stylist were touching me up, and the videographer was filming. They had to wait a few seconds before they could sit on the couch. When the videographer finished getting his shots Tanya sat on the bed. I knew something was wrong right away. She was frowning and staring off into space. I leaned over and gave her a hug. I tried consoling her as much as I could. The videographer lurked in the background and filmed us interacting with each other. I just wanted to transfer any joy in my heart to hers. I wanted her to be happy. She smiled a few times during our conversation, but the energy was just...off. I understood that she was grieving the loss of Angela, that was a lot to deal with emotionally. But...my spirit told me it was something else wrong with her too.

"You okay?" I asked.

"I'm fine," she replied sharply.

The vibes she gave me felt too familiar. But I just ignored it, like I always did. I kept trying to make her smile. Whatever she was feeling inside would eventually surface. I just left it alone and focused on meeting the President.

It was time to go. Daria made sure that I had my journal. I couldn't wait for the President to sign it. My nurses took me downstairs in my wheelchair. We were being transported to the secret location in ambulances. My staff said it was the safest way to get us there. My father was about to catch his flight. He had to start his new job in Wisconsin soon. We took a couple of pictures together before he left.

It was weird to see myself in a wheelchair. But, I was happy that we captured the moment. I wanted to bring my dad too, but he had to leave anyway. Besides, he didn't care that I chose Mick. He thought he deserved the chance to meet the President as much as I did.

As the paramedics were placing me in the back of the ambulance the worst thing happened. I had a flashback that electrified my unconscious. I remembered staring at my bloody legs against the backdrop of the ambulance door. Then suddenly, I forgot how to breathe. I gasped and wasn't able to release it. Tears ran down my face, but I wasn't able to make a sound. I clenched onto my stretcher and rocked back and forth. For a moment, it was June 12th, 2016 again. I felt like I returned to the night of the shooting. My brain told me that I was still in danger, and I started hyperventilating.

"Patience, we need you to calm down," a paramedic said.

My brother Mick leaped into the back of the ambulance immediately. They told him that he couldn't be in there. But seeing his face was the only thing that made sense.

"You alright sis, just breathe, just breathe," Mick said trying to calm me down.

"You can't be in here sir," a paramedic said.

"No, please let him stay," I cried.

"I'm right here, sis. I'm not going nowhere," he said holding my hand.

"He's okay!" Daria shouted.

They decided to let him stay. After a few deep breaths, I came back to reality. Although I was excited to meet President Obama, my fear outweighed any other emotion. The flashback scared me but realizing that I could have more flashbacks terrified me. I didn't want to have a moment like that again.

The President of the United States doesn't just show up to every shooting that happens. His visit helped me realize that I survived something historically tragic. I survived something that I probably shouldn't have. The media called the Orlando shooting the worst terrorist attack since 9/11. I couldn't believe that I actually survived the worst terrorist attack since 9/11.

When we arrived at the secret location, reporters were lined up across the street so I guess the secret location wasn't so secret. Instead of switching me to a wheelchair my paramedics took me inside on my stretcher. I didn't feel like moving at all.

When we entered the building people were dressed in suits and greeted us. It turns out we were inside the new Orlando Magic's practice gym.

I thought it looked pretty cool. The floors were perfectly waxed, and everything smelled new. There were at least 200 chairs on the court. I was taken all the way to the back of the gym. They parked me right next to Larry who was also in his stretcher. We greeted each other and brainstormed what we're going to say to the president. His foot still looked pretty bad. Although I was shot in my legs the thought of being shot in my foot made me cringe. I was proud of him. He was holding it together so well. He was a trooper, we all were.

Everything was going great, I was super comfortable, and my leg wasn't throbbing anymore. Until the most inconvenient thing happened. I had to use the restroom. I really tried to hold it, but I couldn't. Using the bathroom became a painful process. Reaching the toilet wasn't even the hardest part. Sitting down wasn't extremely difficult either. It was standing back up that frustrated me the most. I didn't have strong hip muscles. I had been laying down completely still most of the day for several days straight. I was too weak and too stiff to lift myself up without triggering any muscles in my surgery area.

I would have cried if President Obama made his grand entrance while I was using the bathroom. I was determined to go as quickly as possible. I let my care team know, and they rolled me through the gym in a hurry. There were so many people watching me get pushed to the bathroom, I felt embarrassed. It just felt like everyone knew where I was headed.

When we reached the bathroom I had to get out of my bed. In order to reach the toilet, I had to switch to my walker, and actually walk in. I was able to stand up and balance on my walker with no problem. I started to feel a lot of pressure rushing to my surgery area, but it was manageable. I was fine the first three tiny steps, but then I got super fatigued out of nowhere. The gym was a little too warm for me. My underarms started sweating, and I began overheating. I felt extremely dizzy like I was about to faint.

I was moving at the pace of an injured sloth, and I still couldn't make it. That was the most irritating part. My care team kept fanning me down. They tried their best to keep me calm. My frustration grew immensely. I just wanted to run to the bathroom and come right back. But my body said NO. That was my new normal. Anytime I tried to move faster my body reminded me that I was still a victim. I hated being a victim.

"Patience, it's okay," nurse Jodie said rubbing my back.

"I can't do it," I cried.

"Yes, you can just take your time," Daria said fanning me.

"Just take a deep breath," Jodie suggested.

"Just breathe, you have time, don't worry about missing the President," she smiled.

"He's not leaving without meeting you, believe me," she continued.

"Okay," I sniffled.

I focused my energy on reaching the toilet because that was half the battle. Each step I took moved me an inch closer. I had to take several breaks, but I kept inching until I finally made it. I wobbled into the stall and stood over the toilet. Jodie held my dress up for me as I sat down. I could barely go because I had an audience. When I finally finished Jodie helped me stand on my feet. She was another MVP that day. I really appreciated her for having patience with me. I wasn't the easiest person to deal with at the time.

I washed my hands and inched my way back to my stretcher. My care team helped me lay down. I didn't want to move again for the rest of the day. My leg was throbbing out of control. They rolled me back inside the gym. Even though I successfully used the restroom I still felt like I failed. I tried to hold back my tears, but I felt completely hopeless. Some people in the crowd noticed that I was crying and started encouraging me out of nowhere.

"It's alright," a woman said.

"You got this," another person added.

I smiled at them. We were all in the same room for the same tragedy. They were in pain just like me. But thankfully, they decided to offer uplifting words to me when they needed some also. I was extremely grateful. Whenever I reached my lowest point, God always found a way to let me know I wasn't alone.

My right leg was extremely agitated after using the restroom. My entire leg was swollen, even my foot. I had to take my shoe off because it created too much pressure. It felt like my foot was going to explode. I wasn't allowed to have any more pain medicine, because I took some right before leaving the hospital. I prayed the swelling would go down before the president came. I didn't want to greet him with one shoe on.

A solid 45 minutes had gone by, and President Obama still hadn't arrived. His white house staff told us that he was running late. We completely understood, he was the president of the United States, he probably had a lot to do. The wait just made our excitement grow even more. He was literally going to walk through the door at any moment. I pictured him strolling in with a huge smile. Butterflies swirled in the pit of my stomach. I was extremely nervous and still didn't know what to say to him. Then suddenly, without any fancy introduction, he entered the room with Vice President Joe Biden at his side. We had no idea he was coming too. I was completely shocked. We all gasped, then became ghostly silent and stood to our feet.

"Please sit," Obama said waving his hand.

As soon as we sat down he began his speech. I listened closely to each word. He spoke in a very calm, and sincere tone. He spoke for about 20 minutes, explaining how sorry he was for everything we had gone through.

"If there's anything you need, just let me know," he said.

His words caressed our troubled spirits like silk. His speech didn't seem rehearsed, it was very genuine. It felt like he really came to embrace us, and let us know that everything would be okay. He stepped around the podium and started speaking to people in the first row. Vice President Joe Biden did the same thing. They actually spent time with each family and gave them the opportunity to ask questions. They started in the front of the room and worked their way to the back. There had to be at least 200 people there, but they met with each person. They hugged them, shook their hand, and held them close as they cried.

I was in the back of the room with my care team, Mick, Tanya, and her mom. Angela's immediate family stood in the front. I watched President Obama hug Angela's mom, and shake her father's hand. I watched Vice President Joe Biden encourage Amir, and hug little Ayan. I kept watching them get closer and closer. Each time they took a step I became more nervous. I couldn't help but smile. A horrible tragedy led to that moment, but I wanted to be happy about it. I needed to be happy about it.

I was determined to stand and greet them. Although my swelling didn't go down, I stood tall. I leaned on my walker, and gently placed my right foot against the ground. Anything was better than lying helplessly on the stretcher. I refused to be a victim at that moment. It took a while for them to reach us, but I was ready. I had my book of dreams nearby, with a pen right beside it. It was finally happening. President Obama spoke to Ms. Claire first. Tanya went on the other side of Angela because she wanted to meet him last. Before I knew it he was headed my way. I held onto my walker tightly. Watching him walk toward me was surreal. I blinked and he was standing in front of me.

"How are you doing?" he said leaning in for a hug.

His voice sounded like it did on TV.

"I'm good," I said nervously. I was smiling from ear to ear.

"You know, you all look so nice, if I experienced what you all did I'd look a mess, but you look amazing," he said.

"Thank you," I laughed.

"You're missing a shoe I guess," he joked.

I totally forgot to put it back on. I told myself I wasn't going to forget and I did.

"You know what…we got the wrong shoes on right now," I said smiling.

115

I realized what I said didn't make any sense, but I was just so nervous.

I couldn't believe the president cracked a joke on me either. I couldn't help but laugh.

"But can you sign my book," I said abruptly.

I didn't exactly ease my way into it, but I didn't want to waste any time. Jodie was already holding it right beside me. I was so nervous I could barely get my words out.

"Can you, Can you just…sign the front?" I babbled.

"Of course," he said cheerfully.

I passed it to him with my trembling hand. But before I could give him the pen, he reached into his jacket and pulled out a black permanent marker.

"Oh, you have your own marker," I joked.

"Yeah, I keep a few on me," he chuckled. I couldn't believe I made President Obama laugh.

After signing his name he paused for a moment, then started writing something else. I turned around to find Daria but was already behind me taking pictures.

"Heyy!" I said smiling into the camera.

"Heyy!" she giggled.

When he finished writing he handed me back the journal with the marker still inside.

"Thank you so much," I said graciously. I held the journal close to my heart.

"It's no problem," he said.

Unfortunately, I almost burst out laughing in his face right after that heartfelt exchange. Mick was standing right behind him making silly faces at me like he always does. Before he moved onto the next person I made sure my brother got the chance to speak with him.

"Can you meet my brother Mick?" I asked politely.

"Where's Mick?" he asked.

"He's right behind you sir," someone shouted before I could answer. I pointed to him.

The president turned around, shook his hand, and gave him a hug.

"How are you holding?" Obama asked.

"I'm alright, I'm alright," Mick replied trying to sound cool. He was trying so hard that it was comical.

"You looking after your sister?" Obama asked like a father.

"Yeah, definitely," Mick replied nervously. He never let Obama's hand go.

"You better be," Obama said sternly.

"Oh yeah, got to sir," he replied.

He finally let his hand go. It was funny seeing Mick so nervous. I giggled the entire time.

"You guys still in school?" Obama asked.

"No, not me sir," Mick replied.

"I go to NYU in New York," I said proudly. Then I realized he probably already knew that NYU is in New York.

"What are you studying?" he asked.

"Media, Culture and Communication," I quickly replied.

"Excellent, that's a great place to be, New York," he responded.

"Yeah, I love New York, but I always wanted to explore DC," I said.

"Well, you guys can get a tour, just talk with one of my staff," he suggested.

"Okay, you said it not me!" I laughed.

He gave me another big hug.

"Come on let's take a picture," he said.

He had his own photographers, but my care team had their iPhones ready. We took a few pictures together before he told Mick to hop in. He didn't have to tell him twice, believe me. Then, the funniest thing happened. Mick had my brother Terrence on the phone and asked the president to say hello to him. My jaw dropped to the floor. I didn't know whose idea it was, but it made me laugh. Thankfully, President Obama was super cool and took the phone. He even had a full conversation with him.

"You're lucky to have a brother like Mick," he joked before saying goodbye. He probably thought we were super funny (or super lame).

We finally let him move onto the next person. I laid down on my stretcher and reminisced about what had happened. I was floating on a cloud of happiness. There was no amount of swelling that could steal my joy. I picked up my journal and smiled. Obama wrote, "Dream Big Dreams" on the cover. I never even told him I called it my book of dreams. What a crazy coincidence.

Lesson #6: Focus on the positive.

8

Turn for the Worst

There was a surprise waiting for me when I returned to the hospital. My older brother Kel was there! I was so happy to see him. I didn't think anyone else was coming.

"Bro what are you doing here?!" I squealed.

"You know I had to come to see you, you doing okay?" he asked.

"I'm doing great!" I smiled.

Kel and I never really got a chance to bond. So I was looking forward to spending time with him. His surprise visit meant the world to me. Mick rubbed in the fact that he missed his chance to speak with President Obama. Kel would have done the same thing Terrence did for sure. But he didn't seem to care. He was just super happy that he made it before I got discharged.

Later that same day I had a PT session. It was the PT session of all PT sessions. I had to prove that I was 100% ready to be discharged. But the bathroom fiasco at the Orlando Magic's gym wasn't exactly a good sign. In fact, it was a clear sign that I wasn't ready to go home. I was okay using my walker, I wasn't good. But my physical therapist challenged me to walk using my crutches only. I knew that I was going to fail the test right away. I didn't feel secure using my crutches at all. I was terrified of falling and hurting my leg even more. Thankfully, my nurses promised they wouldn't leave my side. Knowing that made me feel more comfortable.

I desperately needed to get cleared for discharge. I really didn't have a choice. Mick and Kel weren't able to stay much longer. And I refused to be a burden on Ms. Claire. So I tried my very best. Unfortunately, I could even take one full step. I kept trying to move my right leg, but I couldn't. It hurt entirely too much.

"Come on Patience, you can do it," a nurse said.

"I can't," I replied. I started to give up already.

"Just one step at a time, come on," she pushed.

I took a deep breath and gave it all I had. I tried to remember everything my physical therapist taught me. I moved the bottom of my crutches ahead of me and pressed my underarms down on the pads. I gripped onto the handles, drove the crutches into the ground, and pulled myself forward.

"Ah!" I grunted.

I completed a step, even though I almost fell over.

"There you go, sis!" Kel cheered.

"You got this sis!" Mick added. They were recording my PT session so I could see my growth afterward. I regretted asking them to do that.

"Keep going," another nurse said.

"Okay," I nodded.

I wanted to keep going, but all of a sudden I forgot how. I tried to do the exact same thing again, but it wasn't working. I couldn't find the rhythm and started to get frustrated.

"Just relax Patience, it's okay," she said.

"I just can't," I replied. I sunk my head deep into my shoulders. I was ashamed.

"Yes you can, just focus," she replied.

I tried to focus, I really did, but I wasn't able to move an inch. I didn't know what was going on with me. I became angry at myself for getting overwhelmed. This wasn't the girl I knew. Patience didn't give up. Patience was strong and could handle anything life threw at her. This new girl was unfamiliar, she was weak and I hated her.

"I can't do it!" I cried sinking deeper into my crutches. My left leg started to give out.

"Remember, rely on your crutches, not your legs," a nurse said.

"Don't worry, you're not going to fall," she assured me.

She looked me in my eyes and said, "We got you."

I tried again, and again until I finally did it. I almost fell over a second time, but my nurses caught me. I was too tired to keep practicing, so I called it quits. I wasn't proud of myself for giving up. I hated feeling like a weak victim. Unfortunately, my body could only do so much. No matter how much I wanted to rush, the healing process wasn't something I could control. I felt like my doctors weren't going to discharge me the next day. I didn't even show myself enough reason to let me leave. Once they were done testing, I laid back down.

I was very drained emotionally. I asked my brothers to pass me my care packages. I started sifting through my care packages to take my mind of how I felt. I received letters from people all over the United States. And the ones that stood out the most were from a local Orlando elementary school. They sent me beautifully decorated handwritten letters. Each one had a custom note. One letter said, "Dear Hero, we hope you are well," another letter said, "I hope that you are never harmed again." They even added a hand-drawn kissy face emoji. I was extremely touched. Seeing those letters helped me remain positive, and focused on getting better. I eventually put everything away, and started talking to my brothers.

We stayed up all night talking about all sorts of things, movies, celebrities, our siblings, even aliens. However, the most important topic we covered was our mom. It was never an easy conversation to have. I started off by explaining how the shooting impacted my life overall. Then I explained how terrifying it was to almost die without knowing our mother's whereabouts. They were on the same page as me. And wanted to figure out what really happened twenty years ago when our mother first disappeared.

It just didn't make any sense to us. My face was plastered across newspapers, and TV screens everywhere. I expected my mother to recognize me, then give me a call. Unfortunately, I was in the hospital for five nights. If she didn't call by the sixth day, she wasn't planning on it. I couldn't understand how a mother could see her child in pain, and not reach out. It didn't seem logical to me. Something had to be wrong with her, or she had to be neglecting us on purpose. I didn't want to give up hope. So I held my breath waiting for her to contact me. I didn't know when or how, but I believed she would. I needed my mom, even if she didn't need me.

* * *

It was the early morning of June 17th, 2016. My primary doctors just entered my room with a wheelchair. My surgeon sat next to my bed holding papers in his hand.

"Do you honestly think you're ready to go home?" he asked sincerely.

I didn't answer right away, because I was contemplating if I should lie or not. Truthfully, I wasn't ready to go home. I didn't feel safe using my crutches to walk. And I definitely couldn't maneuver up and down a staircase with them. But I lied anyway, and I lied with a smile. I assured him that I was 100% ready to go home. I said the crutches really did help me a lot. Then, he asked if I had any family or friends that would be willing to look after me. I lied again, and I did it with an even bigger smile. I said of course and named a bunch of people. But honestly, I didn't know for sure. Ms. Claire had her own daughter to worry about. Mick had to go back home to South Carolina. Kel had his own life and problems. My father was in Wisconsin, and my long lost mother still hadn't called. So I couldn't guarantee that anyone was going to be there for me. He believed me anyway, I think.

"Okay, well we're going to let you take your wheelchair, and your walker home," he grinned.

"You'll be able to move around a lot faster with your wheelchair," he continued.

"Thank you so much!" I squealed.

I felt like I had just won the lottery. I knew the wheelchair was the only way I was going to be moving around at all. It had the best leg extender, it kept my leg supported. I was so glad that I could take it home with me. It was essentially my lifeline. There was no way I was going to survive without it.

Saying goodbye to everyone was hard. My care team felt like a family. Daria, Jodie, Ms. Jackie, Ms. Sharon, Ms. Karlie were my angels. I never felt compassion like that before, especially not at a hospital. A part of me wanted to run far from Orlando, but another part of me wanted to stay in the hospital for as long as I could. It was unrealistic, but I dared to dream.

It felt like the entire Orlando community wrapped their arms around me. It seemed as if everyone knew my pain without asking. And knew exactly how to embrace me without explanation. They understood the magnitude of what I experienced because they were there. I was worried that I wouldn't receive the same care in Philadelphia. Philadelphia was home, but it didn't feel like it most of the time. I felt severely displaced ever since my grandmother passed in 2012. She was the only mother I knew. She was mean, but she was mine. I knew that she'd always be there for me no matter what. When she died I felt extremely vulnerable. I felt like I didn't truly belong anywhere. Then, all of a sudden, being a "Pulse nightclub shooting survivor" gave me a sense of belonging to the Orlando community. A sense of belonging I've never felt back at home.

My brothers decided to ride with me to the airport. Tanya and her family were meeting me there. I had a ton of care packages to take home. People sent me extra clothes, toiletries, food, stuffed animals, and more. I was extremely appreciative, but there was no way I could take everything on the plane. I had to leave some stuff behind.

My nurses wheeled me downstairs. I wore a pair of red sequin slippers that Ms. Karlie gifted me along with a travel bag set. My brothers said I looked like Dorothy from the Wizard of Oz. It was a corny joke, but I laughed anyway. I wish all I had to do was click my heels three times to return home. Instead, I was bound to a wheelchair and being lifted into the back of a van.

It was about 10 minutes into the ride when my cellphone started ringing. It was a Washington, DC number. I didn't know anyone in Washington, DC so I answered hesitantly.

"Hello?" I mumbled.

"Hi, is this Patience Carter?" a woman asked.

"Yes, this is her," I replied even more cautiously.

How did she know my name? I thought.

She was an official with the U.S. House of Foreign Affairs. And wanted to know if I'd be willing to be a victim's representative. I was selected to speak about the shooting before the committee at their next hearing. I was skeptical because I didn't know anything about politics. But she explained that I'd only be sharing my story. My story was supposed to show the humanistic side of the heated debates around foreign policy. I accepted the offer. she said she was going to be in touch. I hung up in disbelief. I couldn't believe they chose me to speak.

"You'll never believe what just happened," I said.

"What?" Mick replied.

"What happened?" Kel questioned.

"The white house just called me," I smiled.

"And they want me to speak at their next hearing," I said.

My brothers were flabbergasted. They congratulated me and we all got really mushy.

"It's only the beginning, sis," Mick said.

* * *

I arrived at the airport before Tanya and her family got there. My brothers waited with me until they came then headed back to the hotel. They were leaving Orlando later that day. I started to miss them already.

Even though I left behind a ton of care packages I still had too much stuff to carry. Ms. Claire was bringing the suitcase that I packed for vacation too. I knew that we were in for trouble.

Everyone showed up about 10 minutes after me. They had a ton of stuff as I thought.

"We're going to have to throw some of this stuff away," Ms. Claire suggested.

"Yeah, that's fine with me," I agreed. I already knew it would come to that anyway.

Tanya couldn't help carry anything, she was in a wheelchair just like me. It fell on Jim and Ms. Claire to gather everything. Angela parents and little Ayan had their own luggage. They even had to carry the bag that Angela packed for vacation. They had enough to deal with. Ms. Claire and Jim went to check-in our luggage. It took a while because they needed a sticker for each bag. Then, they had to wait in the long line to check the bags on top of that. We were starting to cut it extremely close. After they checked the bags we took off.

Everything started going downhill. We were already running late for our flight, but TSA was taking extra safety measures that day. It was for good reason, but we were in danger of missing our flight. Going through TSA was a nightmare. It was so much chaos because there were a lot of people leaving Orlando at once. The TSA officer directing our line forced Tanya to get out of her wheelchair.

"Can you walk?" he said loudly. It was like he was yelling at her.

"She's been shot in her side, she can't walk!" I yelled.

"Can't she go through in the wheelchair?!" Ms. Claire said.

"It's for security reasons if she can walk she has to get up," he said firmly.

"What?!" Ms. Claire shouted.

"You know what...it's fine," Tanya said lifting herself up.

"I don't even wanna..." she mumbled.

We were baffled. They actually made her walk through the scanner. I could see how painful each step was for her. I was so frustrated. We were the victims, but they made us feel like criminals.

"Can you walk?!" he said loudly again.

This time he was looking at me. I ignored him.

"She can't walk at all, she was shot her in legs. Both of them," Ms. Claire sharply darted out.

She looked down at me and asked, "Where's that paper that the doctors gave you?"

"I have it," I said passing it to her.

It was a note confirming that I had a metal rod in my leg. My doctors said that I should keep it with me whenever I travel, because I may set off the scanners.

"Okay, we're going to have to wipe you down," he said handing the paper back to Ms. Claire.

They took a small white piece of paper and swiped my hands. They placed the sheets of paper in a machine and ran tests. It was taking a while and I was getting more frustrated. We were definitely going to miss our flight. The airport was so huge, and we could only move so fast.

The second we were cleared by TSA we kept moving. Not only were we late, but we still had to catch a shuttle bus to reach the gate. I just knew there was no way we were going to make it. Ms. Claire was running at full speed as she pushed me through the airport. I wanted to cry so badly. She was under a lot of stress, and it was nothing that I could do to help her.

By an act of God, we made it. Apparently, the TSA officer let our flight know that we were running late so they held it for us. It was a huge relief, maybe he wasn't so bad after all.

I had to switch to my crutches to board the plane. Ms. Claire placed my wheelchair next to a stroller that was being checked as well. I started making my way one agonizing step after the other. I tried my best to keep my cool because overheating wasn't going to help.

"It's okay, take your time," a female flight attendant said.

Ms. Claire was right by my side making sure I didn't fall.

"You got it," she added.

The flight attendants definitely had their work cut out for them that day. I was an emotional ball of fire that could only make one full step every 5 minutes. Needless to say, I delayed the flight even more. I finally reached the aisle, then the worst thing happened.

"I'm so sorry, but we don't have any aisle chair that has a leg extender," a flight attendant said.

"You're going to have to try and make it with your crutches," she said.

Ms. Claire started rubbing my back immediately. It was like she already knew I was about to lose it. I felt my eyes watering but I tried to hold back my tears.

"Okay," I said taking a deep breath.

I was already fatigued from boarding the plane. I didn't know if I could make it down a narrow aisle to seat 20 something.

"Can she get a closer seat?" Ms. Claire asked. I was thinking the same thing.

"We already cleared out the entire row so she could prop her leg up," she replied.

Crap. The only way I could get to my seat was by walking. The main thing I couldn't do well with crutches. I regretted lying to my doctors. There was only one thing that hurt more than physical pain, and that was public embarrassment. I hated feeling embarrassed in front of people. I stared at a plane full of passengers who were ready to take off an hour ago. Passengers who had been delayed because of me, the crippled lady. And I had to wobble past all of them trying my best not to topple over on their heads.

I was doing okay until I wasn't. After the fifth step, I just gave up. I scrunched up my bloated face and lowered my head in shame.

"I can't do it," I cried.

I couldn't hold back my tears anymore. I was probably making the ugliest faces, but I didn't care.

"I just can't," I continued.

"Yes, you can just take your time," Ms. Claire said softly. She was right behind me holding me up.

"I can't," I cried harder. I was slumped over my crutches in the middle of the aisle. I was extremely frustrated at how long it was taking me to reach my seat. I nearly ran to my seat on the way to Orlando. Now I barely made it three steps without getting winded. It was a harsh new reality for me.

"Take all the time you need!" someone shouted.

Passengers began clapping and encouraging me out of nowhere.

"Don't worry about it, just take your time sweetheart!" someone else added.

I looked up at them cheering for me, and I couldn't help but smile. They didn't know me, my name, or what I experienced at Pulse. They just saw me crumbling and decided to help lift me up. It was humanity at its finest. I felt a little better. I sniffled a few times, then raised my head. I was a shaky, trembling, wobbly mess but I eventually made it. I squeezed in the row and passed my crutches to the flight attendant. I eased my way down and rested my leg on the seat.

"Alright," I said calmly. I was emotionally drained.

I strapped myself in, took my pain medicine, and patiently waited for departure. Ms. Claire, Tanya, and Jim were finally able to sit down and relax. I took a few deep breaths and let myself sink into the seat.

Then suddenly, there was a mind-blowing announcement that filled the airwaves.

"Due to a storm that's developing in the forecast, this flight has been delayed for two hours," a flight attendant said.

"Unbelievable," I mumbled.

"We're going to need everyone to exit the plane," They added.

"Oh my God!" Ms. Claire shouted.

After all that rushing, fussing, and fighting, our flight was delayed anyway. I took that as a serious sign. Maybe we weren't meant to go home. I was worried that the plane would crash, or terrorists would be waiting in Philadelphia to finish the job. And the last thing I wanted to do was move. A male flight attendant came over to me.

"We're going to let you stay on the plane," he said.

"Oh thank God!" I cheered. That was music to my ears.

"Yeah, that would be entirely too much," he added.

"Too much," Ms. Claire agreed.

He took a deep breath and asked, "Were you guys in that shooting?"

"I hope you don't mind me asking," he added.

"Yeah," I answered.

"Omg, I knew you guys had to be from that, I'm so sorry," he said.

"Thank you," I replied.

I didn't really know what else to say.

"If you guys need anything just let us know," he continued.

Food quickly crossed my mind.

"Do you have any snacks?" I asked politely. I was pretty sure they did.

"Yes, of course, I'll bring you guys some," he offered.

I was glad I asked. Luckily, the plane departed sooner than two hours. I fell asleep as soon as we took off. The medicine knocked me right out. But shortly after dosing off, I had another harrowing experience. I woke up screaming because I heard a loud gunshot in my head. It was like it went off right by my ear. I jumped too hard and strained my leg.

"Ah!" I said bracing my immobilizer.

"Are you okay?" Ms. Claire asked. She was sitting in the seat in front of me.

"Yeah, I just had the scariest dream," I replied.

My heart was racing, and my hands were trembling. I wasn't in any danger, but my mind felt like I was. It was the first time I ever woke up screaming from a nightmare. I prayed that it would be the last. I silently stared off into space until I passed out.

* * *

We finally arrived at the Philadelphia airport. All I wanted to do was get in my wheelchair and go home. But when the flight attendants went to grab it for me…it wasn't there. It was one bad situation after another.

"What do you mean it's not there?" I asked.

I was completely puzzled.

"It must have gotten left in Orlando," a flight attendant said.

"How did it get left?" Ms. Claire questioned. She was just as confused as I was. We just had it.

"Did you check the wheelchair in?" she asked.

"We didn't know we had to check the wheelchair," Ms. Claire replied.

I started crying right away. Ms. Claire needed my wheelchair more than I did. She already went out of her way to help me, because my family wasn't there. The last thing I wanted to do was make her life even harder. But there was no way I could make it through the airport without my wheelchair. I prayed that the airport had one I could use.

I struggled to exit the plane just like I struggled to board it. No surprise there. It was really unfortunate that the most important piece of medical equipment I had was left behind. But luckily, my walker made the flight. At least I thought I was lucky. The minute I began using it I overheated. The exact same way I overheated at Orlando's Magic gym. Sadly, I was under more pressure this time. I wasn't surrounded by a team of medical employees who were paid to assist me. I was surrounded by Tanya's family, a group of people who already had enough to deal with. They were walking behind me on the boarding bridge as we left.

"You guys can just go around me," I said somberly. I was moving negative three miles a minute and showed no sign of moving any faster.

"It's alright, just take your time," Mr. Arthur said.

He was always super nice to me.

Ms. Claire was right by my side guiding each step.

"You got it, just keep going," she added.

I could always count on her to push me. Unfortunately, my body was giving out. I wanted to keep going, I really did. I just felt too weak, and my hip muscles were on fire. I paused, took a deep breath, and closed my eyes. I felt myself falling apart on the inside, but I tried to regain composure. Before I knew it my lips were quivering.

"I can't do it!" I cried.

The words exploded out of my mouth, and my shoulders sank into the floor.

"Just calm down, don't worry about anybody else," Ms. Claire said patting my back.

"Just keep going, take all the time you need to,"she said.

I never felt so defeated in my entire life. I couldn't stop crying. Tanya's family eventually accepted the offer to walk around me. There were so many emotions running through me. Frustration, anger, sadness, self-pity. What did I become? I thought. A victim, a terrified, traumatized, and immobilized victim.

I made it out eventually. Angela's' parents didn't leave us, they were standing there waiting for us to come out. But that made me feel worse. I didn't want to hold them up too.

Ms. Claire said, "Y'all may as well go ahead, she's not going to be able to make it to the car with her walker."

She was right. Nevertheless, Angela's parents decided to wait anyway. I sat on a bench and rested my bad leg on the chair across from me. My frustration grew as I waited for the airport staff to bring me a wheelchair. I was in a lot of pain, my leg throbbed uncontrollably.

I needed a wheelchair with a leg extender that could be adjusted high enough to support my immobilizer. We expressed that to the airport staff over and over again. But somehow, they kept bringing me wheelchairs with leg extenders that were too low. I tried to maintain composure, I really did. However, after the third time, they brought me a wheelchair I couldn't use…I snapped.

"I can't use that!" I yelled.

At that moment, it felt like they weren't listening to me at all.

"She's just upset," Ms. Claire defended.

"The other guys kept bringing the wrong chair," she explained.

Unfortunately, the girl who brought the chair felt super offended and said, "I just go get whatever they tell me, I didn't know."

I felt horrible. Yelling at her wasn't going to fix anything, but my emotions got the best of me. It wasn't her fault that I didn't have my wheelchair. And it wasn't her fault that I couldn't walk. I made sure that I apologized to her. She didn't deserve any of that.

Unfortunately, my problems continued. It was a cloud of negative energy that suffocated me. We went to baggage claim once they finally brought a wheelchair I could use. Angela's parents and little Ayan went to get their car. Ms. Claire did the same. Tanya and I were in matching wheelchairs facing each other by a window. Jim was somewhere nearby. For some reason, Tanya and I began a discussion about the Orlando police department. I'm not sure who sparked the conversation, nonetheless, it resulted in a fiery screaming match.

"They just took too long," Tanya said shaking her head. I agreed with her.

"I know, how did it take three hours?" I questioned. My attitude was already fuming. I was miserable, angry, and in excruciating pain. On top of that, nothing was going right. From the delay at the airport to my wheelchair being left in Orlando. It was just a bad day for me overall. I just felt like being angry.

"And, I just think like…" I paused.

"If the police hadn't pulled me out of the wall like that…" I paused again.

"And just drug me through the grass, would my injury be as bad?" I grumbled.

"I don't know…" Tanya replied hesitantly.

She turned towards the window.

"They could have carried me or something," I complained.

"Like, what made them think that dragging me was the best thing to do?"

I said bracing my immobilizer as sharp pains ripped through my leg.

"Yeah…" Tanya responded softly.

Then, I added the icing on the cake by saying, "I think I should sue the police."

Tanya whipped her head around like an agitated parent and stared at me.

"What?!" she snapped.

"Why in the hell would you sue the police?!" she yelled.

"That's just how I feel, that's my opinion, it took too long and I don't like how they got me out!" I replied. I couldn't understand why she was getting so upset.

"They are the ones who went in there and got us! I was with you until you said that dumb shit!" she yelled.

I squinted at her and shouted, "Are you serious right now?!"

"Dead serious. Like, that doesn't even make no sense!" she screamed.

"You don't even understand the level of pain I'm right now! I can't even walk right now!" I yelled back.

At this point we were already screaming at each other.

"I was shot too! I wasn't shot in my legs but I was shot!" she screamed.

Jim rushed over and asked, "What's wrong?"

"Her!" Tanya screamed.

"Talking about she wants to sue the police?!" she scoffed.

"My leg is NEVER going to be the same!" I screamed.

"You just don't get it!" I cried.

Tanya stood up and hovered over top of me.

"My cousin died! And you don't think I understand pain?!" she screamed.

"You're still alive! My cousin is dead!" she cried.

"I held her in my arms! I have pain too!" she yelled.

Ms. Claire and Angela's parents pulled up just before things got out of hand.

Jim ushered Tanya towards the automatic door and said, "Come on, calm down."

"No! She's selfish!" she screamed.

"How am I selfish?!" I cried.

"We're all in pain, you're not the only one!" she yelled walking away.

"I never said that!" I yelled.

Ms. Claire heard us yelling and came inside.

"What in the hell is going on?" she asked.

"They were arguing," Jim replied.

"She just makes me so mad! I'm done!" Tanya screamed.

"She only thinks about herself!" she said pointing at me.

"Like what?!" I cried harder.

How could she tell me that? I thought.

Ms. Claire took her to the car. Jim grabbed the luggage and loaded the truck.

"Mom, I don't even want to be in the same car as her!" she yelled.

Her anger was growing by the minute. Whenever she got heated like that it was hard to cool her down.

"Well, what you want to do?" Ms. Claire asked.

Tanya just shook her head.

"What happened?" Mr. Arthur asked.

Angela's parents were in shock.

"They were arguing about something," Ms. Claire explained.

She was completely stressed out.

"I'm going to get in the car with them because I just can't," Tanya said walking towards their car.

If I had known my comments were that provoking I wouldn't have said them. I never wanted to upset Tanya like that. She was like my sister. We've fought before, but not like that. At that time, I didn't fully understand why she responded the way she did. I never wanted her to feel like I didn't care about her pain. But I guess that's the way I came off.

I was still sitting inside the baggage claim. Ms. Claire wheeled me to the car and helped me sit. I explained everything to her the best I could. But there was no justification for our behavior. Especially not after surviving a mass shooting together. It was a disappointing moment for us. Our relationship only went downhill after that, and you could probably understand why.

* * *

It took a good night's sleep for me to realize that I was wrong. I was being selfish. When I said Tanya didn't understand my pain, she took it as her pain didn't exist at all. But that wasn't the case. Nonetheless, it was a careless and insensitive thing to say to another trauma survivor. She experienced a level of pain that I could never understand. She held her dying cousin in her arms. I saw her pain. It was foolish of me to insinuate that my pain was any greater than hers. We were both hurting and needed someone to lean on. Unfortunately, Tanya wasn't trying to hear any of that. When we got back home she slept in her mother's room, and I slept in hers.

The next day was worse than I could've imagined. Ms. Claire tried to help resolve the situation, but it only made things worse. It just resulted in another screaming match. I remember Tanya sitting across from me in her room. I was sitting on her bed, and Ms. Claire was standing at the door.

"Go ahead and talk," Ms. Claire said folding her arms.

"I don't have anything to say," Tanya said. Her face was frowned. It seemed as if she already emotionally left our friendship.

"Well, I'll start by saying that I'm sorry. I didn't mean to make you feel like your pain didn't matter. That's not what I meant to do at all," I said sincerely.

"But you always do that," she quickly responded.

Her words caught me by surprise.

"You always make everything about you," she continued.

I didn't agree with her one bit. I understood this one incident, but to say I behaved like that our entire friendship was bogus.

"I really don't see how you could say that," I said trying my best to stay calm.

"You're just selfish, that's it. You only think about yourself," she replied firmly.

I started to get emotional. There were countless situations where I put Tanya's feelings before mine. Her words crushed me. I felt slapped in the face. The level of animosity she had towards me felt completely unfair.

"Out of all people, you would call me selfish?" I questioned.

The word selfish became a trigger word for me. I hated that word.

"You were talking to me like I wasn't shot too like I didn't watch my cousin die!" she said getting upset.

143

"That was my like my real sister!" she yelled.

"Tanya, calm down," Ms. Claire interjected, and stepped into the room.

"No, like I'm tired. She always acts like everything is supposed to be about her," she replied.

"I told you that I didn't mean for it to come out like that. I just wanted you to understand my pain at that moment. As to why I said what I said about the police. You took it like that!" I explained.

"Patience, you just always act like you're the only one going through something. You're just selfish, and I'm just done with it at this point,"she said.

It felt like she was using that moment to address other unresolved issues we had. All the unresolved issues that I ignored in the past.

"I just don't understand how you could call me selfish though, and now you're saying you're done?" I replied.

I started to tear up a little. I was watching our relationship fall apart right before my eyes. I thought back to the night of the shooting. When Angela and I made it out of Pulse, Tanya was the first person on my mind. Going back in for her wasn't even a question. However, if the tables were turned, I wondered if she would've done the same for me.

Tanya kept going. She was getting more and more upset. Ms. Claire tried to facilitate the conversation, but things were boiling out of control. I had enough of her calling me selfish.

"I went back into the club for you! And I'm selfish!?" I yelled.

144

"You couldn't save me! You're not my hero! There was nothing you could do to save me!" Tanya yelled back.

"Calm down!" Ms. Claire shouted.

"No, she always making it seem like she came back to save me!" Tanya yelled.

I was heartbroken and extremely confused. During this time, the media posted articles calling me a hero for going back into the club for Tanya. I guess she was referring to that.

"That's the point! I knew I couldn't save you! And I went back in for you anyway! I went back in just to be with you! Regardless, if I was going to die or not! But I'm selfish!?" I screamed.

All of a sudden, Tanya leaped towards me as if she was about to hit me. Ms. Claire grabbed her.

"Really?!" I yelled.

I was shocked.

"You can't do that to your friends, Tanya!" Ms. Claire yelled.

"I just wish it was her!" Tanya said pointing at a picture of Angela.

"Not her!" she cried pointing at me.

She didn't have to complete her sentence for me to understand what she meant.

Ms. Claire took her out of the room and gave her some time to calm down. I never realized how toxic our friendship was until that moment. Everything escalated so quickly, it was hard to process. How did it get this far? I thought. I had to erase everything from my memory right away. I wanted to love her, and I wanted her to love me back. So I defended her inside. I told myself that she didn't really mean what she said. I told myself that she would never hit me. I told myself that she's still grieving the loss of her cousin. I told myself that she was still my friend. But one question kept crossing my mind: Would you have come back for me? I never asked her.

Tanya and I had an unhealthy friendship. The truth is we stopped being good friends once we got back to Philadelphia. It was rocky, at times, it felt like she was just pretending to be my friend. Although, I didn't want to believe it. I genuinely cared for her. So I kept trying to reconcile. We survived a mass shooting together. I felt like we were supposed to be friends forever. However, the arguments we had before and after the shooting poisoned our friendship. It took a while for me to understand how much.

I didn't know what to do. Tanya came and apologized for jumping at me. We had a conversation about everything and put it aside. At the end of the day, we were still living together. She even said, "You're like my sister, you think I would just have anybody in my house." Her saying that always made sense. She said that I didn't have to leave. If she really wasn't my friend, why would she let me stay at her house? Why would she act as if she liked me if she really didn't? I thought. Nonetheless, just like every other alarming flag that happened in our friendship, I ignored it. I loved her more than our problems.

It wasn't all bad. Tanya and I had a lot of good moments too. We talked about the shooting together over and over again. Talking about the shooting with her was very therapeutic for us both. We watched lifetime movies together like old times. We even did live TV interviews

146

together talking about our survival. Even though we had all that drama going on behind the scenes we still told our story together. As long as she was willing to be there for me, I was willing to be there for her. Even when some of Angela's immediate family started blaming Tanya for her death, I defended her. The issues we had going on with each other didn't matter to me. The fact that Tanya was being blamed for Angela's death was clearly wrong. A gunman entered Pulse nightclub, not Tanya. I didn't understand why they were blaming the victim, instead of the terrorist that pulled the trigger on all of us. People grieve differently, but I couldn't make sense of it all.

The sad part is, Ms. Claire and Tanya visited Angela's family every single day. They even took me over there a few times, because they didn't want to leave me in the house alone. They ate, reminisced, laughed, and cried together. It never felt like her own family was harboring resentment against her for what happened to Angela. I felt sorry for Tanya, even if she wasn't a true friend to me during that time. I still had her back.

The boiling point was at Angela's funeral. Right after Angela's funeral was over, a fight broke out. I was inside a car waiting to drive to Angela's burial. Then, all of a sudden, I saw Tanya snatch off her jewelry. She began charging after one of her cousins. Before I knew it everyone was swinging on each other. It looked like Tanya was getting jumped by her own family. It was a horrible sight to watch. I tried my best to get out of the car. I managed to place my one crutch under my arm and hang onto the car door. I saw a girl about to hit Tanya, so I launched my crutch at her. I missed her, so I launched my other one. I missed again. Then, out of nowhere, a man ran over to me. All I remember was his first coming towards my face. I got punched really hard, but I didn't fall. Jim started fighting the guy who hit me. Luckily, someone helped me get back into the car.

Jim told me that I was punched by one of Tanya's male cousins. He also told me that he beat him up good for me. He didn't respect any man that put their hands on a woman. I was glad he had my back. I called my siblings and let them know what happened. Unfortunately, most of them lived in South Carolina, and Kel was at work. Luckily, one of my brothers showed up, Dominique. He met me at the burial site. I told him that everything calmed down already, but I was happy he came. He made me feel safe. And to my surprise, I later learned that Amir, Angela's brother tried to fight his cousin for hitting me. It made me wonder why he cared enough to defend me. Nonetheless, I was appreciative of him standing up for me.

After the funeral fiasco. more problems came. There was a clear divide between Tanya's family. Ms. Claire, Tanya, and Jim were on one side. And Ms. Nicole, Mr. Arthur, and all of Angela's close aunts were on the other side. No one was talking to each other, or seeing each other. Tanya was still being blamed for Angela's death. Things got so heated I thought they were going to fight again. I never witnessed anything so devastating in my life. I watched Tanya and Ms. Claire fall apart… again. They lost Angela, and then they lost even more family because of pointless drama.

They were such a close family before Pulse happened. They were experiencing trauma after trauma, and I was there witnessing it all. I told Ms. Claire that both sides should have a group conversation to squash things. Unfortunately, she felt like there was too much damage done to be repaired. It wasn't my fight, but I felt sorry for them.

Lesson #7: Maintain the light you have inside of you.

9

Trauma Reveals Trauma

I was at Ms. Claire's house. Tanya slept upstairs in her mother's room. The energy between us was off. I slept in her room as usual. The whole situation had me depressed. I couldn't sleep so I stayed up watching TV. My phone started ringing out of nowhere. It was an old friend of mine.

"Hey, Riley," I answered hesitantly. We hadn't really spoken since I became friends with Tanya. Riley never liked Tanya, she always thought she was jealous of me. But Tanya never liked Riley, because she thought there was something wrong with her. There were times when I questioned Riley, but we had been through so much together I couldn't completely cut her off.

However, I definitely distanced myself from her. I truly cared for Tanya, and I didn't want to be around anyone talking bad about her. But the history between Riley and I goes deeper. Deeper than anyone could have ever imagined. Which is why I answered in the first place.

"So I guess you got your five minutes of fame now," she quickly darted out.

I felt the aggression in her voice radiating through the phone.

"What?!" I sharply replied. I had no clue she was going to come at me like that.

"Yeah you heard me, you're milking this whole situation, acting like you're better than everybody," she said.

Her words stole the air from my lungs. I didn't know if she was under the influence or if this was just how she really felt. The conversation started off so crazy I didn't even know how to respond.

"Are you kidding me right now?!" I yelled.

I felt my heartbeat rising faster and faster. This couldn't have been the Riley I knew.

"Don't get loud me with me, because you know I can beat your ass!" she shouted back.

I was stunned. This was exactly the Riley I knew. She always lashed out on other people like this for no reason, but I never thought she'd do it to me. At first, I laid there in the bed in disbelief. Then I sat up and really tried to make sense of it all.

"What is wrong with you?!" I yelled.

"Are you really serious right now?!" I screeched at the top of my lungs.

Riley always had her issues, but this was beyond strange, even for her.

"Yeah whatever! Don't get loud like you can beat me!" she yelled.

"What?! I can't even walk!" I screeched again.

I'm pretty sure the entire neighborhood could've heard me.

"You're all on TV acting like you're better than everybody, bitch you're not better than nobody!" she screamed back.

I couldn't understand where her hostility was coming from. I hadn't spoken to her in a long time, but I never wrote her off. I had a connection with Riley that I never wanted to relive again. I didn't want to bring it up, but she had clearly lost her mind.

"I can't believe you!" I cried.

"After everything we've been through!?" I cried even harder.

I slid to the side of the bed and planted both feet on the floor. I grabbed my walker and stood up.

"I can't even walk right now!" I screeched again.

I switched over to facetime. I wanted her to see me crying and standing there with the walker. I thought she might come to her senses. It didn't change anything at all.

"You're talking about five minutes of fame and I can't even walk right now!?" I screamed while pointing the phone down to my legs.

"Keep fucking yelling like you're tough! You know where I live and I will definitely send you my address!" she yelled.

Nothing she was saying made sense. It was like she wasn't even listening to me. She was more concerned about me yelling than what

151

I was saying. I couldn't help but yell. I was hysterical because I didn't understand why she called me with that energy. Riley was one of my best friends before I met Tanya. We've gone through hell and back. I couldn't understand what made her snap on me like that.

I heard footsteps coming downstairs.

"Why are you talking to me like this?!" I screamed.

"I was shot in both of my legs! My femur is shattered and you're talking about fighting me!?" I questioned.

"Enjoy your five minutes of fame bitch!" she yelled back.

"How can you say that to me?!" I cried uncontrollably.

I was holding the phone in one hand, and hanging onto my walker with the other. Ms. Claire and Tanya walked in.

"What in the hell is going on?" Ms. Claire asked.

"What's wrong?" Tanya questioned.

"Who's on the phone?" she said grabbing it from me.

"It's Riley!" I cried. I was crying so hard I could barely make words.

She was still sitting there on Facetime emotionless.

"Hello?!" Tanya said to her.

"I don't know what she gave you the phone for, she knows where I live," Riley continued.

"First of all why are you even talking like that?!" Tanya snapped.

"She keeps screaming at me like she can beat my ass!" Riley yelled.

"After everything we've been through!" I screeched in the back-ground.

"After everything we've been through!" I screamed again.

My eyes were closed shut. I was screaming from the bottom of my soul.

"Calm down baby," Ms. Claire said rubbing my back.

"Sit down," she said ushering me back onto the bed.

I couldn't stop crying.

"You know what we're not even going back and forth," Tanya said hanging up the phone.

"I can't believe she would talk to me like that!" I screamed.

I felt so much old pain rushing back into my spirit. Memories that I wanted to burn and hide forever were flooding my mind and I couldn't stop crying. I didn't even cry this hard when I was shot. Being shot hurt less than what I was feeling at that moment.

"Okay just calm down," Ms. Claire said consoling me.

"You can't let her get you upset like that, she ain't nobody important," Tanya said sincerely.

She sat down on the bed next to me.

"You don't understand…" I whimpered.

I tightly closed my eyes trying to push back the painful memories that were haunting me.

"What do you mean?" Tanya replied.

I slowly turned to look at her. Then closed my eyes again.

"You don't understand what we've been through together," I sobbed.

I couldn't hold in the secret that I had been keeping hidden since I was 17 years old.

"What happened?" Ms. Claire asked.

"It's okay you can talk to us," Tanya said.

I didn't want to have to say it. But I just couldn't hold it in anymore. I wanted them to understand why Riley had the power to upset me so much.

"She's the only person that knows my deepest pain…" I cried.

"I can't believe she said all that stuff to me…" I cried harder.

"What happened?" Tanya asked again.

"I…we had…" I paused.

I couldn't bring myself to say it. I started wailing at the top of my lungs. Then I took a deep breath and let it out. I knew I could trust them.

"There was this guy who tricked us into doing stuff…" I sobbed.

"Oh my god…" Ms. Claire mumbled.

"Into doing what?" Tanya asked sincerely.

"First it was just pictures…" I started.

"He told us all we had to do was take pictures and then we'd get money," I shared.

I couldn't stop crying.

"But then he threatened to show the pictures to our families, and school if we didn't keep doing what he asked!" I screamed.

"Oh my god, it's okay, it's okay," Tanya said embracing me.

"She's the only one that understands…" I cried.

"I can't believe she would" I started wailing extremely hard again.

I didn't want to revisit that painful time in my life. It was the scariest, and longest, three weeks of my life. I was young, naive, and easily manipulated. I tried to run far away from that part of my past. But my heart couldn't keep it tucked away anymore. I had new trauma, on top of other new trauma, on top of old trauma.

If I didn't open up to Ms. Claire and Tanya about my experience that night, I would have killed myself. I would've waited until they fell asleep, then killed myself. I would've grabbed my walker, quietly. I wouldn't have grabbed my crutches, they'd make too much noise. I would've inched my way into the kitchen to grab a knife, the long slender one. I would've slowly made a U-turn, really slow. Then I would've inched my way into the bathroom, as fast as I could. I would've closed the door behind me, gently. I would've looked in the mirror and cried for a little bit. I would've pictured every horrible moment I've ever experienced. I would've pictured it twice, just to remember how painful it was. Then I would've sat down on the toilet and pushed my walker aside. I would've taken a deep breath, then another. Then one more. I would've inhaled deeply on the last one. I would've cried again, way harder than I ever have. I would've conjured up enough painful memories to finally do it.

I would've stabbed myself in the stomach, one good time. I would've stabbed myself in the stomach because I didn't know that slitting my own wrists would've worked faster. I would've felt stupid, the most stupid I've ever felt. I would've felt sad, really sad. I would've felt sorry, really sorry. I would've regretted stabbing myself. And I would've been too ashamed to call for help. I would've sat there on the toilet dying, dying slowly. I would've taken everything to the grave, literally.

When Riley called me with so much anger in her heart, I was extremely hurt. We never had big issues in our friendship. We only stopped talking, because I became friends with Tanya. I thought she was the only person in the world that would never cause me any pain, because of what we experienced together. When the truth is ready to come out, it just does. Without any permission from you. No matter how scary or ugly the truth is. One reminder of that experience made me want to end it all. But talking to Ms. Claire and Tanya about it made me feel better. They listened, they embraced me and showed me how much they truly cared. I felt like I bonded with them on a new level. I felt safe with them. I felt like I could tell them anything.

Lesson #8: Running away from your trauma will never heal it.

10

A Patient Road to Recovery

D uring all of that chaos, I didn't spend any time on truly healing from Pulse. I was too busy fighting, yelling, screaming, and adding more pain to my trauma. Ironically, I didn't realize how dysfunctional my life had gotten until after being punched in the face. I had no peace in my life. And I couldn't even run away from it all. I felt like there was no one I could turn too. I held a lot inside during every interview. I wanted to give people hope, but I barely had any for myself. I wanted to show them that there can be a quality of life after a tragedy, but everything in my life was completely horrible. I felt like I was drowning in agony all of the time. Both physically and mentally. I didn't know what to do.

In the midst of it all, I finally decided to focus on healing. You can say it was long overdue. I was making other people's problems my problems. And that extra stress wasn't healthy. I had two soul provoking revelations. One morning I woke up and Tanya wasn't there. I was in her room all alone. I had to pee urgently, but my walker was too far from the bed. Although it was just a few inches away from me, I still couldn't reach it. I leaned over as far as I could, but it wasn't enough. I felt so useless. I called Jim on my cellphone and asked if he could come to move it closer. He didn't have a problem with it since his room was right next door to Tanya's. When he came in and saw how close the walker actually was to me, he burst out laughing. His laugh made me laugh too, and lord knows I needed a good laugh. But deep down inside I was petrified. What if Jim wasn't home? What would I have done, peed on myself? I thought. It was a sharp moment of awakening for me. I needed to get better as soon as possible.

My healing went beyond physical pain. I had a lot of mental healing to do as well. One early afternoon, Tanya and I fell asleep on her bed while watching TV. All of sudden, I woke up screaming at the top of my lungs. I heard a loud gunshot in my head, just like I did on the plane. It felt ghostly real. My body was sweating, my hands were shaking, and my heart was racing out of control. Once I realized that it was just another flashback, I began to cry. Tanya was still asleep so I woke her up.

"What's wrong?" she asked.

"I thought ...I heard a gunshot," I cried.

I felt ashamed to even say it.

It was a "this again?" kind of moment for me.

"Oh Lord..." she replied.

"I thought I rolled on your leg or something," she joked.

I smiled a little, but I was extremely frustrated. I was tired of being a victim. I hated having moments like that because it made me feel weaker. Weaker than my hip muscles that quivered uncontrollably each time I moved.

"Why would he do this to us?" I questioned.

"I don't know..." she said shaking her head.

The gunman was dead, but my fear of him was alive. And that fear was growing day by day. That fear haunted me, and I had enough of it. The nightmares were becoming too much for me. I made a conscious decision to heal that day. I took a deep breath, and said "No more." I repeated it over and over again in my head until I believed it. I didn't want to be trapped in that club forever.

I started journaling that same day. I grabbed my book of dreams and wrote about what happened. I kept journaling every day. Sometimes I forgot to write on my good days. It just seemed like writing on my bad days were a lot easier. And I had a lot of bad days.

* * *

Sorting through all of my healthcare paperwork was challenging. Luckily, Ms. Claire helped me understand everything properly. I was grateful for her guidance. My dad was never any help with that sort of stuff. When it came to college applications, and FASFA I had to figure it out on my own. I made monumental mistakes. One time I lost all of my scholarships because I didn't know my dad had to fill out some forms. Unfortunately, NYU's deadline for the forms had passed. I received an email the next day saying that all of my financial aid for that year was rescinded. I reached out to every NYU president, vice president, and dean I could contact, begging for help. Luckily, they understood the mix-up and I got my financial aid back. I couldn't afford to make any huge mistakes with my healthcare papers. With Ms. Claire's help, it didn't take long to get everything sorted out.

I had home-care therapy in the early stages of my recovery. It only lasted for about four weeks. The physical therapist came to Ms. Claire's house to clean my wounds, change my bandages, and prick me with needles. I had to get needles in my stomach every day for the first month to prevent any bacterial infections. The needle was half the size of my index finger. They were brutally annoying, but not unbearable. One day, Ms. Claire had to do it for me, and it made her cringe. She did it though, but I couldn't watch it.

Home-care therapy went pretty well. I learned how to walk with my crutches for real this time. But first I had to complete several strength building exercises. I practiced standing leg lifts. It sounds easy, but my legs felt like sandbags at the time. While I lifted one leg, I'd be standing on the other. I couldn't fully stand on my right leg so I put most of my weight onto my walker. My therapist said that I needed to apply more pressure on my legs, especially my bad one. It was the only way it could get stronger. That was a foreign concept to me. I was taught that if something hurts to leave it alone until it doesn't anymore. However, this new journey forced me to change my old way of thinking.

I remember doing a stair exercise outside of Ms. Claire's house. My physical therapist wanted me to practice walking up stairs. But they weren't regular stairs. They were hard, rigid, cement stairs. I was scared out of my mind. My physical therapist stood behind me the entire time for support. But staring at the ascending stairs freaked me out. I didn't really believe that I could do it, but my therapist kept assuring me that I could. So despite my fears, I gave it my all. And I actually made it up to the first step with no problem. I turned around and smiled at my therapist in excitement. That was my first real sign of significant growth since returning home.

I felt super motivated and kept crutching up the stairs until I got tired.

I was so excited that I almost fell. My therapist grabbed me and made sure that I was okay. It startled me a little, but it didn't crush my spirit like it normally would have. Instead, I felt accomplished. It felt good to know that my fear of falling was the only thing holding me back, and not my leg itself.

I wanted to walk on my own again. I wanted to wear heels again. And I wanted to move freely without any pain again. Nevertheless, those goals were extremely big, and so far from my reach that I couldn't even look forward to them. It was depressing to think about the long road of recovery ahead. So I stopped thinking about it. Instead, I focused on reaching smaller milestones. Like getting my immobilizer removed, and being able to plant my feet firmly on the ground. The one thing I always hated was feeling stagnant. But setting smaller goals that I could reach sooner kept me motivated. It kept me hopeful.

The human body amazed me. Each time my nurse removed my bandages for cleaning, my bullet holes were smaller. Whenever I felt like I wasn't getting any better, my wounds showed me otherwise. It was inspiring to watch my body restore itself from the depth of trauma it had been through. I was glad that I witnessed it. Seeing those holes closing made me feel powerful, and proud. I felt like I could bounce back from anything.

* * *

It was the beginning of July. It was going on a month since the shooting. I was finally starting outpatient therapy, and I was looking forward to more progress. My sessions took place at the Penn Musculoskeletal Center in West Philadelphia. My insurance covered a van service to take me to my appointments, but it didn't work out in time. The process of setting up the service took too long, and I had a strict therapy schedule. Thankfully, Ms. Claire volunteered to take me to my doctors' appointments. There were a lot of people saying "if there's anything you need just let me know," yet I had a hard time believing those people.

I didn't understand why so many people cared about my wellbeing all of a sudden. Those family members I hadn't spoken to in years, those former teachers, those reporters, those organizers, etc. I didn't believe that any of them meant what they said literally. I know they meant well, but I didn't trust that I could truly call on any of them if I seriously needed help. Getting to my doctors' appointments and therapy sessions were serious. I didn't have time to rely on anyone that I couldn't fully depend on. There were only a few people that actually cared about me before I was shot. And it was already hard enough asking them for help. I had a thing for suffering in silence. Although, I needed all the help I could get.

The thought of rushing to class in New York with crutches was terrifying. My goal was to head back to NYU in the fall without needing them. It was an ambitious goal, but I was determined. And I was on track. I had an evaluation once my home-care therapy sessions were over. My primary doctor took an X-ray of my injury. He was happy to show me how well my fracture was recovering. My femur still looked pretty jacked up to me, but I took his word for it.

"Well, I think you can take that immobilizer off now," he smiled.

"No way," I replied. "Seriously?" I turned to look at Ms. Claire in disbelief.

"Yes absolutely! You've shown a lot of improvement!" he said.

"I got to capture this," I joked.

I grinned at Ms. Claire and asked her to take a picture of me holding my immobilizer in my hand. It was a big moment for me.

"You so silly girl," she laughed.

I handed her my phone and started I unstrapping my immobilizer. I held it next to my face and smiled as hard as I could. I almost forgot my doctor was there. I just hated my immobilizer so much. I couldn't wait to yank it off. Ms. Claire took a few pictures, and I posted them on Snapchat immediately. After my mini photoshoot was over, it was time to get back to business.

"You should focus on applying more pressure, and stretching," he said sincerely.

"You have to start stretching rigorously, it's very important," he added.

"Okay," I replied.

I hated stretching but my doctor made it very clear that it wasn't an option. The fate of my leg depended on it. If I wanted to get back to normal stretching was the only way to get there. My doctor told me to walk around the office on my crutches. I had to get comfortable with bending my knee. It was so tight.

"Just keep applying a little more pressure each time," he insisted.

"Okay, so just tap the ground?" I asked.

"Yes, just gently touch the ground with your foot," he said.

"You don't have to do too much, but you want to start activating the motion," he continued.

"Oh ok, gotcha," I replied.

I felt so much lighter without my immobilizer on. It made walking on my crutches a lot easier.

"You know something funny?" I asked Ms. Claire.

She was standing in front of me as I walked.

"What?" she replied.

"I made all that fuss about the wheelchair and I don't even use it," I chuckled.

"Hmm, it's sitting right there in the living room," she smirked.

* * *

My sessions at Penn were extremely challenging. Luckily, my physical therapist was patient and kept reassuring me that I was capable of doing all the exercises. He introduced me to using light weights and resistance bands. I was much stronger than I was before but I didn't know if I could handle weights.

I never really worked out before the shooting. So working out while I was injured felt insane. I lacked the confidence I needed to give it my all right away. My first exercise was leg raises with a five pound ankle weight while lying flat on my back. It doesn't seem like much now, but I was terrified back then.

"Trust me Patience, you can do this," my physical therapist said.

"I wouldn't hurt you," he assured me.

"I don't know..." I replied hesitantly.

My biggest fear was lifting my leg and the whole thing falling off from the femur down. I had a metal rod and screws that held everything together but I didn't want to test it out. Plus, it hurt like hell to lift my legs without weights, so I wasn't looking forward to adding them.

"Just give it a try, come on," he insisted.

"Okay," I said.

I tried to lift my bad leg up but the weight was too heavy. "I really can't," I said.

I felt defeated instantly.

"Ok, let's try one more time," he replied.

I tried raising my bad leg again but I still couldn't get it up. I really tried.

"I can't," I said. I felt myself getting emotional.

"It's okay, I'm going to take you down to two pounds, and see how that works for you," he said.

"That's fine," I mumbled.

My spirit was crushed. I hated not being able to do things. It sucked. He switched out the ankle weights and asked me to try again. I almost didn't want to do it, I really wanted to go home. Nevertheless, I knew that wasn't going to help me at all. I tried again and I was finally able to raise the bad leg.

"That one wasn't so bad," I smiled.

"See I told you, let's do four more, you got this," he replied.

He was right. I really surprised myself in the first few sessions. I was amazed at how fast I progressing. I went from a two pound ankle weight to five pounds in no time. Unfortunately, stretching became the hardest part. When I wasn't weight-lifting, I'd be stretching. I had to keep extending my bad leg over and over again. The goal was to sit down and be able to extend my leg completely straight out in front of me. Then I had to hold it for as long as I could. In the beginning, the area surrounding my injury was so tight I couldn't fully extend it at all. It took a lot of stretching at home to really make a great difference. I did a ton of exercises in Ms. Claire's living room while looking at that wheelchair I had a hissy fit about. I became more advanced with each therapy session. I opened up to my physical therapist about my journey a lot.

"I feel so much stronger every time I come here," I smiled.

"That's because you are getting stronger," he said smiling back.

We were doing a standing resistance band exercise. One end of the band was wrapped around my ankle on my fractured leg. And the other end was tied to a pole. I had to lift my leg sideways and backward.

My leg quivered the entire time but I got it done.

"Remember when you first came in, you couldn't get one rep in with these bands, now look at you!" he cheered.

"Yeah, it's crazy...I would have never thought I'd be this much better," I explained.

My growth was truly mind blowing to me.

"You just have to keep putting in the work, especially on your own time at home," he replied.

"Doing the work on your own is going to have you off those crutches in no time," he emphasized.

We transitioned to a new exercise. I had to lay down on the table and turn over on my side.

"Now I know you've been really worried about having a limp, right?" he asked.

"Yeah, that would be awful," I answered.

Having a limp at twenty years old wasn't going to be cute at all.

"Well how seriously you take these leg raises are going to determine that," he said.

"Your leg is stronger than you think, but the limp is determined by your muscles in your hip and thigh region," he continued.

"Each time you make a tiny step, you're leaning, but you want to build those muscles," he said pointing to my hip and hamstrings.

"So you can make a strong step," he explained.

"Okay," I said nervously.

I was a little worried. The fact that I controlled the fate of my walk scared the crap out of me. That was a lot of responsibility for me to bear. I was never consistent with exercising before. It was hard for me to push through. I lacked the will power and motivation to fight through really tough workouts, but now I didn't have a choice. Having a limp or not was dependent on my ability to persevere, and stay consistent. If I didn't succeed there would be no one to blame but myself.

The thought of that made me feel miserable. I didn't want to have that responsibility. I didn't ask to get shot and have a shattered femur. I didn't want to have to fight through any pain. I just wanted my old leg back, my old life back. My old life wasn't any safer than my new one, but at least I could run.

* * *

I wasn't happy. My relationship with Tanya was extremely unstable. Our friendship was on a steep decline. We never fully recovered from the airport argument, her jumping up to hit me, and truthfully, all of the unspoken issues we never addressed. We were still friends, but we lost the closeness we had. I felt it and she felt it. Nonetheless, we were going to be those Orlando Shooting survivors for life so we kept trying.

Unfortunately, most of Tanya's family hated me for defending her at the funeral. Yes, you read that right, they hated me for defending their own family member. It turns out that Ms. Nicole was behind the "Tanya let Angela die" rumor. Crazy but it was true. Ms. Nicole started the fire that burned through their family. Although, the gunman was clearly to blame for Angela's death along with 48 other innocent people, blaming Tanya was just her way of grieving. It's sad, but it was the reality. Now I was left to defend myself against her family, and keep my guard up with her at the same time. Throughout that experience, I learned that every battle isn't worth fighting. I should've invested all of my energy into healing, not defending anyone. Especially when I later learned that there was no one ever defending me.

On top of that, a lot of people stopped checking in on me. My dad was busy in Wisconsin, my siblings were back to their own lives, and other family members only kept in touch via social media. I had over a hundred text messages and calls throughout the duration of my hospital stay. As soon as I left, the text messages and calls dwindled to a halt. A lot of people had my number, but only a few used it. Facebook comments only go so far. I didn't reach out to anyone who didn't care to reach out to me. I changed my number just to see who really cared to have it or not. There weren't too many. There were people who genuinely cared, and people who just wanted to stay in the loop. I learned how to tell the difference, and let things play out on their own. I had other things to worry about.

I was stressed about the possibility of not being able to return to school. My leg was slowly getting better, but if I didn't get cleared from crutches I wouldn't have survived in New York. Attending school was my only way to escape. It was my safe zone, my fresh start. I loved school passionately. I had worked very hard to get into NYU. I kept straight A's in high school and graduated as valedictorian. Finishing my degree was extremely important. It didn't just mean a lot to me, but to my mentors that helped me get there. If I couldn't finish for myself, I at least had to finish for them.

I was under a lot of stress. Among other things, I was terrified at the thought of having to limp for the rest of my life. I was in pain 24/7, and there was nothing I could do about it. I had to keep exercising, stretching, and applying more pressure. It seemed as if life was applying pressure on me too. I was just as shattered, broken, and traumatized as my femur. But life kept applying more and more pressure on me. I guess it was the only way I could get stronger too. But gosh, did it have to be so painful, and did it have to be for so long?

Lesson #9: Don't rush your healing process.

11

No Fairytale

I didn't know if I was ever going to get a break. It felt like I was being forced to heal from everything else outside of the shooting. My mother never surfaced, my past came back to haunt me, conspiracy theorists kept attacking me, my best-friend was distancing herself from me. And the list continued.

I never really had any emotional space to deal with any of it. And I wasn't talking to anyone about it. I was a shaken up soda bottle getting ready to explode. My experience at Pulse put too much pressure on me. That pressure revealed all of the trauma I never healed from. It was way too much at one time. At some point, I just became numb during my recovery. I became numb to everything. I was expecting something else to go wrong every day. I lost more hope, self-love, and confidence. I felt defeated. I wasn't sure if I was healing or dying inside. I was just lost. However, the media gave me a new facade to work with. A new facade to drown my sorrows in. I wasn't just the perfect student anymore. I was the perfect, inspirational, strong SURVIVOR. I was Orlando Shooting Survivor, Patience Carter. I was the girl who SURVIVED a mass shooting and bounced back gracefully. Although, behind the cameras, my experience was far from graceful. People were putting me on a pedestal that I had no business being on. Nevertheless, I let them put me there. I went along with it. I was definitely surviving each day, but I wasn't living. Living shouldn't feel like a burden. But that's what it felt like.

Until Amir came.

He wasn't exactly prince charming right away, but he was nice. He was everything I didn't need to focus on at that time. Which was absolutely perfect. After the shooting, Amir came to Philadelphia to be with his family. He brought his daughter, and Haile again. According to Amir, they were no longer in a relationship. She only came to be there for support during that rough time. It made sense. Amir just lost his little sister, his best friend. He needed all the support he could get. He also explained that they lived together so they could co-parent. Tanya always assured me that they were over several times. I knew she had no reason to lie, so I believed her. It seemed a little strange to me, but it did make sense. They had a baby while they were in college and had to take turns watching her in between classes and basketball practices. It sounded like a lot. Ultimately, Amir living with his baby's mother wasn't a big deal… in the beginning. He wasn't mine and I wasn't his. Unfortunately, you don't ask to fall in love, it just happens. Besides, I didn't really know what I deserved and what I didn't. Both of us came with a lot of baggage. More than the average person would be willing to carry. But love doesn't just make you crazy, it gives you strength. Strength to carry as many bags as you can.

I was in a really broken place when Amir and I started talking. And so was he. He was a trauma survivor just like me. I felt his pain, and he felt mine. He was battling demons on top of everything else, just like me. Demons that he couldn't tell anyone about, just like me. We just understood each other in a way that no one else did at that time.

He always went out of his way to talk to me. Even with Ms. Nicole not liking me anymore, and his family wanting my head on a stick. He always made me feel special no matter who was around. I didn't know I loved him yet. I just knew there was something special about him. Something changed from the moment I looked at him from my hospital room bed. There was something deeper about his eyes. The way he looked at me, it felt spiritual. However, things got messy, quick. And I mean really quick. Ms. Claire and Tanya brought me over Ms. Nicole's house. First of all, I was shocked. In the early aftermath of the "Tanya let Angela die" rumors, the hostility seemed to die down. I still had my immobilizer on during that time. It wasn't too long after the funeral brawl. But things seemed okay. Tanya wasn't fighting her cousins anymore. And Ms. Claire wasn't squaring up with anyone either. There was even a new rumor that surfaced right before they reconciled. Ms. Nicole accused Tanya and Ms. Claire of vandalizing her car. She posted pictures of it on Facebook and directed the caption towards them. Ms. Claire and Tanya were even more hurt by that outrageous accusation, but I guess they got over it.

Ironically, things seemed back to normal overnight. Tanya told me that she did a TV interview with Ms. Nicole about Angela. And that they had a 'good talk' in their uber ride back home. Those were her words exactly. Then all of a sudden, they were all cool again. It seemed pretty mutual too. It looked like Ms. Nicole accepted Tanya back into her heart as well. Even Ms. Claire seemed like she was able to forgive Ms. Nicole for the foul things she said about her daughter. It was definitely an unusual situation. The last time I checked there was "too much damage done," and Tanya and Ms. Claire were crying their eyes out. But I was happy to see them working things out. It was just strange to me. I stayed out of it though. I learned my lesson after getting punched in the face.

While I was over Ms. Nicole's a super awkward situation happened.

Amir had been talking to me the entire time. He was helping me up and down the stairs. And he was making me smile a lot. It was obvious that we liked each other. Everyone could see it as big as day. I was sitting on the couch with my leg propped up on the table. I couldn't bend my leg at that time. Amir came into the living room and sat down next to me. Right next to me! I thought he was crazy. But then a few seconds later he put his arm around me. That's when I thought he had lost his mind. We weren't even dating.

"Um…Are you sure you want to do that?" I whispered to him out the corner of my mouth.

"Yeah, why not?" he replied defensively.

He was such a Leo.

"I mean, listen, I don't want-" before I could finish he cut me off.

"I am not in a relationship with anybody, I'm grown, man," he explained.

"Okay…" I said awkwardly.

I took his word for it. But I felt the energy change in the room. Quick. I felt like everyone was staring at us on the couch. Especially Ms. Nicole. After that nothing was ever the same. Ironically, Ms. Nicole gave me a plate of food anyway. I wasn't sure if she poisoned it or not, but her food was so good I was willing to take that chance. I didn't know how deep her dislike was for me. And her giving me a plate of food definitely took me for a loop. Everything was strange, too strange for me.

Amir and I fell head over heels in love with each other really fast. Falling in love in the midst of so much tragedy was beautiful. He was my safe place. However, the love we shared came with a hefty price tag. And it seemed like I was the only one who had to pay.

Amir spent just about every single day at Ms. Claire's house until it was time for him to go home. And if he wasn't there we'd be on the phone for hours. It seemed like the closer we became the farther Tanya pushed me away. She was giving me the silent treatment a lot. Then she started bringing her other best-friend around every day. Her energy was off whenever Amir and I spent time together. I noticed how she changed, but I admit, I didn't care. I was being selfish. Amir made me happy, the type of happy that I hadn't felt in a long time. It was refreshing to just be happy. So I took as much as I could. Amir was headed back to Florida soon and I didn't know what was going to happen to us. But I knew I wanted to make the best of every day I had him. Even if it meant pissing Tanya off with our lovey-dovey nonsense. I just prayed she understood.

And she did. She always gave me an attitude but she always came around eventually. We talked and I understood why she was upset. She told me that I was putting Amir before her, and Amir was also spending most of his time with me, and she didn't appreciate it. It was an unfair situation for Tanya to be in. Even though she had her mom and brother, she just needed somebody to care about her too. I didn't want to lose her friendship over Amir. So I tried my best to stay neutral when Amir came around. He didn't make it easy though. He was such a charismatic person. Everyone wanted time with him. He helped brighten everyone's day. He was an amazing guy, the life of the party type. It was such a dark time for everyone. And everyone needed his energy around them. But all he wanted to do was spend time with me. And all I wanted to do was spend time with him. It was like we were selfishly addicted to each other. And everyone could see it. It wasn't healthy, but it was delicious. Like fast food on a Friday night. He was the cold fries at the bottom of the bag, and I didn't want to share with anybody.

Unfortunately, the whole dynamic changed once Amir returned home to Florida. That's when our fairy-tale love bubble popped. The Cinderella stage was over. He was back to living with Haile and their beautiful daughter, in sunny freaking Florida. Nothing he said mattered to me. It didn't matter if they weren't in a relationship. It didn't matter if they were only co-parenting. It didn't matter if he didn't love her anymore. It looked bad, it felt bad, it was all bad. From the inside looking out, and from the outside looking in.

I became insecure, really insecure. I thought Amir still loved Haile and just wasn't telling me the truth. Despite what it looked like, he kept assuring me that nothing was going on. He would stay on face-time with me all day to help ease my fears. But it wasn't enough. Not for him and not for me. He wanted to see me again, and I definitely wanted to see him.

"I want you to come down here," he said in sly Leo fashion.

"I don't know Amir," I replied nervously.

"I don't think I'm ready to travel anywhere right now," I explained.

"What if something else happens while I'm going to see you, and I can't even run," I continued.

"Look, you can't live in fear," he replied.

"You got to get past that or you're going to miss out on life for real," he said sharply.

"If my sister was still here, she wouldn't be stuck in the house hiding," he continued.

I'm sure he was right. Angela seemed brave, way braver than I was.

"You're right," I agreed.

"Plus, it's Florida too, and all the stuff that happened, what if -" I started explaining, but he cut me off.

"I understand all that," he said.

"But Florida is really big. What happened to you and Tanya, happened in Orlando. I live in West Palm. That's hours away from Orlando," he continued.

"Okay...but I'm on crutches though," I said hesitantly.

It was easier to move around without my immobilizer on, but I was still really slow.

"I will come to get you from the airport, you don't have to worry about anything," he said.

"You think I'm going to let something happen to you?" he asked firmly.

I wanted to be a wise guy and say something slick. But deep down inside I knew he would never let anything hurt me. I truly believed that.

"No," I answered confidently.

"Then come on," he replied.

"Alright," I said.

He was smooth, really smooth. Come to think of it, he was too smooth. I didn't need therapy, I had Amir. The smooth talker. I didn't think twice about going to see Amir. I told Ms. Claire and Tanya that I was going and they thought I was insane. I didn't care though. I was in love. Real, reckless, head over heels in love. I gathered up my crutches and hopped on the first plane smoking. Not literally, but it didn't take me long to book a flight and a hotel to stay in. And just like that, I overcame my fear of travel. All it took was love. A real, reckless, head over heels kind of love. He was the Bobby to my Whitney. And I was down for whatever.

* * *

Unfortunately, it was time to pay that hefty price. I became the man stealing whore who vandalizes cars overnight. Yes, you read that right. Apparently, a random source placed me at the scene of Ms. Nicole's car being vandalized at four o' clock in the morning. The story went from Tanya and Ms. Claire doing it to me doing it. According to the imaginary source I was standing on crutches at four o' clock in the morning messing up his mother's car. Yeah, as crazy as that sounds someone actually said it. That was my reality, people saying anything they could to assassinate my character. The second Amir showed any real deep love for me the "destroy Patience Carter" party began. As soon as I went off to Florida, all bets were off. I heard new outrageous rumors about me every single day. It seemed like all of the hostility that was once directed towards Tanya and Ms. Claire made a 360 turn and smacked right into me.

Amir friend's back at home would tell him all of the evil things his mom was saying about me. Amir always told me before I could hear it from anyone else. I had no idea why she decided to turn up the heat on me out of nowhere. She was just giving me a plate of food, and now she was calling me a "home wrecking whore." I began to question myself. Am I a home wrecking whore? I thought. I asked Amir about the same question. And he'd look at me like I was crazy. He kept assuring me that his relationship was over long before I ever came into the picture. He even claimed that he dated other girls before me. I asked Tanya for reassurance as well. She'd look at me just as crazy too. And say that I shouldn't worry about her opinion at all. Maybe I did care too much about what other people thought. Nevertheless, it was a heavy accusation that hurt me deeply. I was a lot of things, but I never ever wanted to be "that" girl too.

* * *

I didn't know if I was healing mentally anymore. My leg was getting stronger, and before I knew it I was cleared from my crutches. But didn't know if I was okay or not. I headed back to NYU in the fall, even though I wasn't sure if I could make it through the year. My limp was becoming less noticeable, and fewer people had the urge to ask me, "What happened to you?" However, I didn't do anything to prepare my mind for the transition. I was too worried about Amir, we were in a dysfunctional long distance relationship. I was too concerned about the things his mother was saying about me. And I was too damaged from my own past to let it go. I just never understood how the rumors came about in the first place. They were so mean and malicious. I felt extremely attacked. Still, Ms. Nicole didn't know me at all. So she didn't have any reason to lie. Someone had to feed the poison to her. I just couldn't figure out what horrible person would try to destroy me like that. Especially at such a fragile time in my life. Why me? I thought. All of that evilness spilled into my relationship with Amir.

Sadly, we crumbled.

It was the wrong time to be in a relationship. I was hurting inside, he was hurting inside, and all we did was hurt each other. Over and over again. It was an endless cycle of negativity. He had his mother in his ear about me. And I had Tanya in my ear about him.

I'd often ask Tanya for relationship advice. But she always told me that I shouldn't be dating Amir in the first place. she said that he was a manipulator. I didn't listen though. I loved him from the bottom of my soul. And I knew he loved me too, regardless if he was manipulating me or not.

Until I went through his phone.

Amir came back to Philadelphia. And I returned from school. He was hanging out with his friends and family. I didn't see him much that day. We weren't exactly in the best place. But Tanya and I were. She was basically coaching me through my relationship with Amir at the time. We were gaining our closeness back. The energy felt good between us so we decided to go out later that night. Besides, there was no way we were going to allow what happened at Pulse to stop us from living our lives. By this time Tanya and I had already faced a lot of fears when it came to being around crowds. We felt like we could handle it. And it was actually a lot of fun.

Amir and his friends got a hotel room. Tanya and I came over after we finished partying. When we got there Amir had a serious attitude with Tanya. I didn't know why. Tanya was so upset that she decided to leave. I told her she should talk to him, but she didn't want to. I was so confused. I didn't understand why the two of them had any problems. When Tanya left, I stayed and talked to Amir about it. He didn't say much to me. Apparently, he and his friends had been drinking so he only wanted to sleep. Something didn't feel right. His energy was off towards Tanya, but his energy was off towards me too. I stopped trusting Amir once he returned to Florida. My biggest fear was him rekindling his relationship with Haile. But little did I know she should've been the least of my concerns.

Amir's cellphone notifications kept going off. Several female names were popping up. I grabbed his finger and placed it on the home button to open it. He was completely passed out so he didn't feel a thing. I scrolled through his messages and learned that he had been flirting with other women. After scrolling through his SnapChat I learned that he had been sleeping with one of his exes that lived in Philadelphia. I had seen her before, she smiled in my face. But surprisingly, that didn't hurt the worst. It was another conversation that he had with a girl who lived in Florida that broke me to pieces. He was telling her things he never told me. Beautiful things, how he wanted to spoil her. How he wanted to give her the best things in life. It crushed me. I screenshot that conversation he had with her and sent it to my phone. Then I smacked him. I smacked him hard as I could. He woke up instantly.

"What the hell are you doing?!" he shouted.

"Who is this?!" I screamed.

"Who is this?!" I screamed louder.

181

His friends were in the room pretending to be asleep. But I knew they weren't sleeping.

"What are you talking about?!" he yelled.

"Calm down!" he shouted.

"No! No! No!" I screamed.

I started throwing anything I could find at him.

"Stop it, Patience!" he yelled gripping me up.

My leg wasn't in Floyd Mayweather condition, but I didn't care. I was livid.

"No! How could you do this to me?" I cried.

I was still trying to hit him.

"Out of all people, why would you do this to me?" I cried harder.

I completely was mortified. We argued and fought for at least twenty minutes before I called Tanya to come back for me. For some reason, I thought Amir could do no wrong. For some reason, I thought he could be perfect. That was my biggest mistake.

* * *

I wasn't perfect either. I started dating someone else right after our hotel fight to get revenge. He was crushed when he found out. I didn't tell him, ironically, he found out after going through my text messages.

182

I'm not sure why I did it. I think I wanted to hurt him worse than he hurt me. However, two wrongs don't make a right. It only added to our problems. Trust was broken on both sides.

We got back together eventually. No matter what happened we just couldn't let each other go. I forgave him, and he forgave me. But we let everything we had been through poison us. Everything was ruined. I remember our final breaking point.

It was my 21st birthday in Miami. I rented a beautiful condo with a balcony and a full kitchen. Everything was so gorgeous around me, but I felt so ugly inside. I was at one of the lowest points I had ever been in my entire life. Amir and I were harboring serious resentment towards each other. On top of that Tanya and I were back to an unstable place. She was tired of Amir and I putting her in the middle of our drama. In addition to that, Amir's relationship with his mother was suffering, because she didn't want him to be with me. I felt horrible because of it. There was so much going on. So I tried to drink all of my problems away that night. Of course, it only made everything worse. But I wouldn't be Patience Carter if I didn't make everything worse.

A few of my siblings were there to help me celebrate, Kate and Mick. Kate and I still had our underlying issues, but we loved each other enough to move on. Tanya brought one of her female cousins with her. Amir originally told me that he wasn't coming. He missed the party bus experience, and I was pretty bummed about it. But he ended up surprising me. As soon as I got off of the party bus, he was standing there in Leo fashion. Apparently, Tanya was in on it. That was very friendly of her.

I felt special, and everything seemed okay. We all knew nothing was perfect, but everyone tried their best to have a good time. It was actually a lot of fun in the beginning. My siblings were having a good time with Amir and Tanya. And I was enjoying myself a lot too. We kept drinking, partying, and turning up.

Things didn't go bad until the very end of the night. I was drunk, really drunk. And I was angry, really angry. Everything I had been holding inside began pouring out. Tanya tried to leave, and I ended up pulling her hair. My sister tried to calm me down, and I ended up swinging on her. I was so depressed that I actually tried jumping off the balcony. Luckily, Mick caught me in mid-jump. I cried for the rest of the night. I had ruined everything. Amir was the only one who could calm me down. He stayed the night to make sure that I didn't try to hurt myself. When I woke up, Amir and I were over.

"You messed up Patience," he said.

I could see the pain all over his face.

"I don't even remember everything that happened," I said sincerely.

I sat up and rubbed my eyes and asked, "What happened?"

I grabbed his hand, but he pulled away.

"You tried to fight Tanya, and you even tried to fight your sister," he explained.

"You even tried to kill yourself," he said placing his hand on my face gently.

"Oh my god, I'm sorry," I said tearing up.

"Now my cousin is mad at me, because I stayed the night with you, making sure you were okay," he said shaking his head.

"Is she here, let me talk to her," I cried.

"No, Patience she doesn't want to see you," he started tearing up too.

"I'm so sorry Amir," I sobbed.

"I know, I know," he released a few tears, and then let my hand go.

"Now what we have," he paused.

"It has to end," he continued.

"Amir, no," I cried.

"No, Please," I cried harder.

"It has too. Everything is too messed up," he cried.

"I will still be here for you, but I have to keep my distance myself, I have to get my head right too," he explained.

My heart instantly broke into a million pieces.

"Amir, please," I begged. "I messed up. I'm sorry, please," I cried.

"I have to go," he said wiping his eyes before walking out.

I wanted to run after him, get on my knees, and beg him to stay. But my siblings were there and I didn't want them to see me like that. They had already seen enough.

* * *

I lost my best friend, my boyfriend, and my sanity all at once. It was for the best. I needed time to focus on truly healing. Amir needed time to actually grieve his sister's death. And Tanya needed a serious break from our mayhem. We never devoted time to repairing our hearts before trying to extend love. So when we tried to, we failed. And when we kept trying to force it, we failed even more miserably.

I was hurting really bad. Yet I still had to finish my semester of school as the perfect, smart, exemplary, inspirational, strong student who SURVIVED a mass shooting gracefully. It was really hard. Each interview I did got harder and harder. None of the reporters knew how crazy, dysfunctional, and unorthodox my personal life had been for the past year. I had to give advice on how to SURVIVE, on how to HEAL, and I realized I was the least qualified person to do so. On social media, I was a guru for survival. I was surviving alright, but I wasn't healing. I was surviving, but I wasn't living.

I thought that I couldn't live without Tanya and Amir in my life. I tried to reach out to them, but they were both ghosting me. It really hurt to know that I was the one who broke the last straw. It hurt to know that I had nothing and it was all my fault. It sucked. Life sucked for at least a good month. Then it got even worse when I found out Amir was dating the girl I caught him cheating on me with. That set me back a couple of weeks. Nonetheless, it was exactly the fuel I needed to pick myself up. It was the motivation I needed to better myself.

I forgave myself. I forgave myself of my mistakes, and I started writing a book. I finished my semester of school. I made new friends. I set new goals, and I was determined to reach them. I tried my best to stop punishing myself for all of the mistakes I made. I already did that enough. I tried my best to move on. Everyone else was. And everyone else seemed happy with their lives. I wanted to feel happy with my life too.

I signed up for a pageant. I needed something extreme to focus on. I applied for UCLA's summer creative producing program. I wanted something to look forward too. I applied for several film internships. I was desperate for a new experience. I even applied for an LA modeling program. I wanted to challenge myself. I was intentionally signing up for things, competing in things, and applying for things just to feel better about myself. And I actually ended up getting accepted to everything. So I had more than enough on my plate to keep me busy.

I was learning how to be happy with myself. I was learning how to accept my flaws. I was learning how to love myself for the first time in my life. I decided to focus all of my energy on actually becoming the person everyone thought I was. I started using my platform as a way to inspire other people who were battling things they couldn't speak about either. I decided to become an open book. I was struggling for a couple of months but I made major progress. I laid a lot of painful things to rest. I was accomplishing new things, posting more on social media, and really starting to feel good again. I wish I could say that my problems ended there, but they didn't. I wish I could say new problems didn't arise, but they did. Life just has its own way of working itself out.

Amir and I ended up getting back together again. I was in LA for my UCLA program and he was in LA starting a business with his friend. I reached out to see how he was doing. I didn't know if he was going to respond or not, but he did. He let me know that he was single. Of course, that didn't really surprise me at all. We kept communicating through text on and off. It wasn't anything too major. I could sense that he had a different mindset. He wasn't as wild as he was before. He talked to me with more care. He embraced me with more love. Love that I truly needed.

Tanya and I became friends again before I got back with Amir. She wanted to do my makeup for the pageant I was competing in. Of course, I said yes. I couldn't wait to have her back in my life. I missed her so much. Two months was the longest we ever went without speaking to each other. I wanted her to forgive me. I never wanted us to go that long without speaking ever again. Thankfully, we became close again. It seemed like everything was really coming together.

Until the problems came, again.

Amir and I were in love like never before. I eventually moved in with him. It seemed like everything we went through only brought us closer together. No matter what anyone said he had my back, and I had his. We were outlaws for life. No one wanted to see us back together. They had good reasons, but we were different people. We were like a brand new couple, mostly. It took a while for me to get used to it. I still had my insecurities, and he had his. We carried some pain of the past with us. It took some time to let things go. Things weren't peachy keen overnight, but it didn't take long for us to build a strong foundation.

The more Amir saw Tanya and I hanging around each other the more concerned he became. He didn't think that I should be friends with Tanya anymore. He kept telling me that he didn't want the problems we had in the past to resurface. My heart was telling me it was something deeper. Something deeper that he wasn't telling me. There had to be more to the story. Why would he feel this way about his own cousin? What did he see that I didn't? I thought. He never revealed it right away. He just kept warning me. Nevertheless, I wouldn't be Patience Carter if I didn't do the opposite of what he was telling me.

So I invited Tanya to LA to stay at our place.

We were on such good terms it felt like old times again. When she came to LA everything was great. Until it wasn't. Apparently, Tanya accidentally left a water hose out of the wall when she washed her clothes late at night. At that time the water hose connected to the washing machine was occupied for business purposes. In order to wash clothes, we had to put the hose back inside the wall each time. Unfortunately, Tanya didn't tell anyone she was going to wash her clothes. It was late at night and we were all asleep. So no one was able to warn her to put it back in before starting the machine. She fell asleep after loading the machine. When everyone woke up, the entire basement was flooded. Tanya couldn't stay to help clean up, because she had to catch her flight home. Everyone else was left to clean up, and pay for the water damages. It was an unfortunate situation, but it added more tension between Amir and her. It was definitely a sign.

I ended up snooping through Amir's phone again. For no particular reason. I had a window of opportunity so I took it. I didn't have any business doing it. Honestly, I didn't fully trust him yet. Luckily, I didn't find anything new. That made me really happy. However, I found an old video that pissed me off beyond measure. I randomly wanted to see what Amir did the day after my birthday. Which was also the day he broke up with me. It turns out that Amir was with the same girl he had cheated on me with. Once he broke up with me he went straight to her. I was livid, but I couldn't truly get mad about it. I was shocked, but not really. He technically broke up with me. He had the right to go and do whatever he wanted. But gosh, the same day? How Leo of him.

I kept looking. Then, I found another video. It was dated a couple of days before my birthday. It was a video of him, Tanya, and the same girl again riding in his car. I was crushed. The video confirmed two things. One, Amir never stopped cheating on me once we got back together the first time. And two, Tanya was well aware, and she even was hanging out with the girl. My friend, my sister. My boyfriend, my heart. How shady of them both. Needless to say, I went off. I confronted Amir immediately.

Amir started telling me everything. For the first time, he actually admitted that he did me extremely dirty. That was a big step for him. Even when he was caught red-handed in the past he never owned up to anything. He would deny, deny, deny even if the evidence was right in my hand. It was the first time he sincerely apologized for everything he had done. He realized that he never dealt with his own pain inside. The pain of losing his sister. He admitted that he didn't know how to be the superman I needed him to be. But he promised me that he was never going to do anything like that again. He assured me that he had grown a lot since we broke up. For the first time, I truly believed him. Not for the things, he said, but for the ways, I already saw his behavior change. I could see that he was becoming a different guy. He was trying to be a better person. So I decided to give him a break. However, I wasn't going to give him anymore. He had one more chance.

I didn't know how I was going to handle the situation with Tanya. I just wanted her to tell me the truth. It was a difficult situation for her to be in. I understood that they were family. It always going to be "family over everything," regardless of right and wrong. Yet I didn't understand why she wasn't transparent with me. She knew I would do anything for her. Even after all of the chaos. Whenever she asked me for money I gave it to her. Whenever she needed to talk I listened. I thought our friendship was mutual. But, one day, Amir finally opened up to me. He explained the reasons why he didn't want us to be friends anymore.

"Tanya's not really your friend, Patience," he said.

His words took me by surprise. This was his own cousin he was talking about. He tried his best to explain everything without hurting my feelings. Back on June 12th, 2017 Angela's high school basketball team held a memorial game in her honor. It was a beautiful event with an amazing turnout. When I got there I saw Amir's new girlfriend holding his daughter. The same girl he had cheated on me with was there. Holding his daughter. Needless to say, I was heartbroken. At the time Tanya was supposed to be my friend. So I started texting her right away. I told her how pissed off I was, and that I needed her to talk to me. Apparently, Tanya read my texts aloud to Amir. And everyone around him was able to hear it. Including his new girlfriend. Why would a genuine friend do that? I thought.

I wasn't sure if Amir was lying or not. Why would he lie on his own cousin? It didn't make any sense to me. However, I was determined to get to the bottom of it. I loved Tanya, and even when we weren't speaking I always stayed loyal. I had too much love for her to betray her. The thought of her not doing the same devastated me. Unfortunately, Amir was able to prove everything he said. One of his friends was there that day and confirmed every single detail. His friend was even willing to involve his sisters because they all heard what Tanya said. His friend swore that Tanya never acted like a real friend to me at all.

I confronted Tanya about everything. I told her that I didn't care if it happened, I just wanted the truth. I wanted her to own up to it so we could move on. A large part of me still couldn't let her go. I knew she was hurting about Angela's passing. I knew she was dealing with a lot, and I wanted to be there for her. Despite what Amir told me, I still cared about her. But when I gave her the chance to own up to the accusations, she denied everything. She denied ever hanging out with the girl and reading my text messages aloud at the basketball game. she said that Amir was lying on her to save himself. But I told her that Amir already admitted his wrongdoings. And I told her that I saw the video of her in the car with Amir and the girl. Sadly, she kept denying everything over and over again.

I didn't understand why she lied to me. I already knew everything. All I wanted her to do was tell me the truth. I would have forgiven her. But she couldn't even do that. I expected Amir to lie, and deny, deny, deny like he always did. Surprisingly, he was the one who had the courage to admit his part. I just wanted her to care enough about me to do the same. But she clearly didn't. I decided to distance myself from her after that. It hurt, but I couldn't trust her anymore. Friends tell the truth to each other, no matter how much it hurts.

* * *

Amir and I ended up moving to Florida together. I took a break from school to finish my book, and Amir wanted to be closer to his daughter. Things with the LA business didn't work out. After the basement was flooded there was too much negative energy surrounding everyone. We all needed some space. Unfortunately, Amir couldn't get any of the money he invested back. His name was never on any paperwork so he couldn't do anything legally. He had to start over from scratch.

It didn't take us long to get on track. It was a little slow but we made progress. We started praying with each other every morning. Amir thought of the idea. I never saw him as the spiritual type. So it really took me by surprise. We were two souls that needed help. Help that we couldn't give ourselves. So we reached out to God together. And prayer changed everything for us. We became closer than ever. Our love reached new heights that nobody could tear down. We gave all of our pain to God. After a while, it felt like God was smiling down on us. It felt like God was proud of us. Everything in our lives started looking up. We even started a YouTube Channel to share the light that we found in so much darkness. We were happier than we had ever been. But there was only one problem. His mother, Ms. Nicole.

She wasn't buying any of it.

The last time she checked, we were over. I knew her hate towards me had to be deeper than her wanting Amir and Haile back together. Surprisingly, Ms. Nicole loved the other girl that Amir cheated on me with. She even let that girl stay in her house. I guess the "home" was already wrecked when she came. So that couldn't have possibly been the reason.

Nonetheless, the hatred ran deeper than I could've ever imagined. Amir's close friend told him that his mother continued her rants. But it wasn't just about me, it was about us. She declared that if we ever had any children together she would never come to see them. she said she would never want anything to do with them. I could handle her saying anything she wanted about me. Hate me, dislike me, judge me, whatever. That was my cross to bear. But I never wanted that pain for my children. I never wanted my kids to feel unwanted. I never wanted them to feel unworthy, or less valuable like I always felt growing up. I wanted my children to have better. I felt like life was coming full circle. I couldn't handle the thought of my kids suffering from the mistakes I made. It was terrifying to think that the generational curse that was passed onto me, was probably going to be passed on to my kids. The same pain, the same mistakes. The same hurt, the same abandonment. I couldn't understand why she hated me that much. Then one day Amir told me. He revealed that Tanya was the source behind all of the rumors.

"I remember her saying, you don't want to be with her, she nasty," he said shaking his head.

"She told you that?" I squealed.

"she said the words 'I'm nasty' to you?" I questioned.

"Yeah, I stopped her before she could tell me anything else," he claimed.

"But she definitely had to tell my mom some really messed up stuff about you," he continued.

"I can only imagine," I said tearing up.

My heart was crushed in a million pieces.

"And when did she say this?" I asked.

"When we were in West Palm Beach," he said.

"Wow," I responded. "Unbelievable," I sniffled.

"My mom tried to tell me some stuff too, but I never wanted to hear it," he confessed.

"Really?" I asked.

"Yeah, I knew it wasn't going to be the truth," he said firmly.

"I knew her source was Tanya," he said.

Tanya and her mom were the only ones that knew about my experience with child pornography. Besides Riley, but Riley didn't know Ms. Nicole. Yet somehow she found out, or heard some twisted version of it. Although, the experience only lasted for three weeks, I was still severely traumatized. It was something I never talked about. It was something I never wanted anyone to know. Nevertheless, that's why Ms. Nicole kept warning Amir about me. She even told him that I have sex with men for money, and places to stay all the time. Amir said those were her exact words to him. I was devastated. It was completely inaccurate. I could deal with other parts of my life being exaggerated and fabricated. I was already used to conspiracy theorists doing that to me online. But I remembered crumbling in that room with Tanya and her mom. I remembered pouring my heart out to them. I remembered feeling safe with them. I didn't do anything to deserve that level of betrayal. I wouldn't wish that heartache on my worst enemy.

All the outlandish rumors made sense. Ms. Nicole only looked at me from the picture Tanya painted. I wouldn't want my son to be with a girl like that either. But that wasn't me. There was so much more to my story. I made a lot of mistakes. I gave my full heart to people who never deserved it. I've been dumb, and idiotically naive growing up. However, the girl she was picturing in her head wasn't me. She had been told lies about my character from the very beginning. From someone who I thought was my friend. And I didn't even know. I never even knew that I needed to defend myself.

Tanya pretended to be my friend that entire time. She called me her sister. But as soon as the "Tanya Let Angela die," rumor started, she threw me under the bus and didn't think twice. The only thing she cared about was getting the heat off of her. She smiled in my face and even gave me advice on how to deal with the rumors. My sister, my best friend was even willing to destroy me to save herself after I was willing to sacrifice my own life for hers. Once again, I gave my all to someone who didn't deserve it.

What if I was the one stuck in the nightclub during the shooting, and she was the one who made it out safe? I've always wondered, would she have come back for me? I didn't have to wonder anymore. The answer was clearly no. I don't regret going back inside for her. That was my choice because that's the type of person I truly am. But I do regret ever thinking that she would have done the same for me.

Amir said that he never told me because he wanted me to see for myself. He said that I needed to learn that everyone isn't really my friend. Just like he had too. Amir had been silently defending me against his mother, and his entire family for a long time. I had to look him in his face and make sense of every single lie he heard. It was heartbreaking for me to do. I regret not being able to tell him about my past myself. I'd rather be judged from my truth than someone else's version of it. Luckily, Amir didn't judge me at all. He told me that he felt sorry for me.

"I don't blame you. I blame your parents and everyone that was supposed to protect you," he said.

He continued, "I wish I could have been there to protect you, but I'm here now."

I hoped he really meant it.

Lesson #10: Love will always prevail.

This world hates love like ours.

I'd hide our love forever
 before I let negativity come near it.

People don't understand love like ours,

196

Because its easier to fear it.

Unconditional love doesn't exist,
  we were the first to premiere it.

I want to scream to the heavens that I love you,
  But the world might hear it.

12

Then Live

After all of that, I survived. And I'm happy to say that Amir and I are getting married. He proposed to me the day after my 22nd birthday. Which totally made up for the day after my 21st birthday. It was the best day of my life. I remember it like it was yesterday.

First, he took me to a fancy nail salon in downtown Miami. There was a beautiful chandelier glimmering at the front door. The service was phenomenal. I was seated right away and enjoyed a stellar manicure and pedicure. I even let Amir pick the color. He picked a bright orange. I was cool with orange. Right after that Amir surprised me with tickets to a Miami Heat game. I felt so spoiled. I just wanted to hug him and never let him go. I didn't think the day could get any better that. But I was wrong. We left the nail salon and headed straight for the game.

The arena was huge. I couldn't wait to see the inside. It was my first time ever going to see a Miami Heat game. I really wanted to go see one since we moved to Florida. To my surprise, we didn't enter through general admission. Instead, we entered around the back. The line was super short. I thought it was so cool. I felt like a special VIP. As soon as we walked in there were performers on a big stage, a bar, and the team mascot. It definitely wasn't general admission. The mascot saw us and he waved, then came over to us on his segway. He did the funniest dance before taking off. It made me laugh so hard. Amir said he didn't plan that part, but I gave him credit for it anyway. The energy was magical between us that day.

We eventually found our seats and sat down. We were in a high section overlooking the arena. I didn't care about what kind of seats we had. I was just glad to finally be there. Then the unthinkable happened.

"You know what. My friend actually just texted me, and told me to come downstairs," he said looking down at his phone.

"What friend?" I asked.

I never knew he had a friend at the Miami Heat.

"A girl I met not too long ago, she works here," he replied.

I never knew he had a female friend at Miami Heat. Given our history, my jealous girlfriend radar was going nuts. However, I played it cool. Thank God.

"Oh ok," I replied plainly.

We started walking downstairs. There were thousands of people in attendance that night. It was a Miami Heat vs. Cleveland Cavaliers game. Everyone wanted to see Dwyane Wade and LeBron James go at it for what could've possibly been their last time playing against each other. The crowd was bananas. We kept getting closer and closer to the court. Amir started videotaping me. He said that he wanted to get some clips for our YouTube Channel. I didn't think anything of it. We were Youtubers. But before I knew it we were standing on the court. Amir spotted his friend.

"Hey Krissy," he said tapping her arm.

"Oh my god hey! I'm so glad you guys are here," she squealed.

"You two won our Kia giveaway!" she shouted.

"No way," I replied in shock.

"This is crazy!" I shouted.

"Look at God, wow," Amir smiled.

I started jumping up and down in joy.

Krissy passed us over to another Miami heat staff member. Everything moved so fast.

"Okay, you guys need to put these shirts on," he said handing us two X- Large gray t-shirts.

"You can just sit here, and when we announce the Kia winners, I'll come to grab you guys," he explained.

I couldn't even process it all.

"Okay!" I said.

I was completely stunned. I couldn't believe what was happening.

"Wow," Amir smiled.

He seemed as shocked as I was.

"We just won a car?!" I shouted.

"No, I don't think so, we won the Kia seat upgrade," Amir smiled.

"These are our seats now," he said pointing at the chairs.

"Oh my God, Oh ok!" I laughed.

I can be really slow sometimes. I took out my phone and started recording. Our new seats were courtside. We could see all of the players, staff members, and dancers. I felt like I was dreaming. I couldn't stop smiling. It was absolutely unbelievable. Now I was positive the day couldn't possibly get any better than that. Until it did.

It was a commercial break. The Miami heat staff member came back for us.

"Alright, guys!" he shouted.

"Oh my God!" I squealed.

My heart was racing. Amir and I stood up.

"You guys are going to stand right there," he said pointing in between two dancers standing on the court.

"Just look up at the jumbotron and wave," he said before quickly disappearing.

"Okay," I grinned. My stomach was in my shoes.

We stood in between the dancers on the court. Amir was so much calmer than I was. I guess he was playing it cool. The energy of the arena was so magnetic. Dwyane Wade and LeBron James were less than 20 feet away from us. And we just won courtside seats! I couldn't hold in my excitement as he did.

There was a huge camera right in front of us. And a few other people standing around it.

"Amir are we supposed to say something? I can't remember," I whispered out the corner of my mouth.

"No babes," he replied.

"Are you sure? What are we supposed to do again?" I panicked. My brain started melting.

Suddenly, the dancer on my right side responded to me, "Just smile and wave into the camera," she grinned.

"Okay thank you!" I squealed.

Out of nowhere, the mascot came over to us again. I couldn't get enough of this guy. He had a flip phone and a briefcase in his hand. I tried my best to look out for the cue to smile and wave. Then suddenly, I heard it.

"Here's our Kia seat upgrade winners!" shouted the announcer.

"Oh!" I giggled.

It was show time. I gave my brightest smile possible. The crowd started cheering for us. We looked so good on the jumbotron.

"Just keep smiling," the dancer reminded me.

I felt Amir slowly leave my arm. Then the dancer stepped away from me too. I was still smiling and staring up at the jumbotron. I noticed that Amir disappeared from the frame. I quickly turned around.

And there he was. Down on one knee. Holding a black ring box with the most beautiful diamond ring I had ever seen. I couldn't react, respond, or even move. The crowd started cheering for us louder.

"Patience, will you marry me?" he grinned in Leo fashion.

I still couldn't react, respond, or even move. I was stunned. If the crowd knew our story they would have been too. I wanted to cry, scream, and laugh all at the same time.

Amir started waving his arm to get the crowd even more excited.

"And the answer is!?" shouted the announcer.

The crowd cheered louder and louder. I felt like I was about to take a game-winning shot.

"Yes," I said nodding my head.

I barely squeezed the word out.

"She said yes!" shouted the announcer.

The entire arena went crazy. Fans were cheering for us as if we played for the Miami Heat. Amir stood up and placed the ring on my finger. He embraced me like he never wanted the let me go. I couldn't believe it.

He knew all of my flaws, and I knew all of his. He'd seen all of my scars, and I'd seen all of his. After everything, we had been through. After all of the trauma, we had experienced. After all of the pain, we caused each other. After so much opposition. We chose love. We chose forgiveness. We chose to learn and grow.

* * *

I wouldn't be Patience Carter if this story ended perfectly. My life was never destined for that. Tanya and I never addressed our issues. Amir's mother still doesn't want anything to do with me, or my future children. My own mother is still missing from my life after 23 years and counting. My dad is still battling with his own demons. My leg still hurts from time to time. I feel super depressed every now and then. The list goes on. But honestly, it's not that bad. At least I'm alive.

I'm finally living in my truth. I'm learning how to love myself. And I'm not looking for any new facades. I don't have to parade around pretending to be perfect. I'm far from that. I'm a diamond with a lot of scratches on it, and that's okay. Take me as I am, or don't take me at all. I walk confidently in my scars. The ones that are seen and unseen.

I could've lost my mind a long time ago, but I'm still here. I could've been killed in that nightclub during the massacre, but I'm still here. I could've taken my own life several times, but I'm still here. I could've been broken, defeated, and destroyed. Yet I'm still here. And I'm standing strong. Not just with two repaired legs, but with a repaired mind. I have a spirit that can't be broken. I have a heart that's full of love. Now that's truly living.

I can't go back, but I can press forward.

I have my siblings. I've gotten a lot closer to them since this entire experience happened. I realize that family is everything. And I'm building a different narrative for my own. I'm sure that if I had the guidance of my older brothers, and sister I would've avoided a few wrong turns. If I had leaned on them more during my recovery I probably wouldn't have had so many problems. I probably would have better judgment when it comes to people. But they're in my life now, and I love them so much.

I have a stepdaughter-to-be. I get to learn how to be a better mother figure through my interactions with her. She teaches me how to be more nurturing. I always thought that I would never be able to possess any motherly traits because I didn't have my mother's love. However, I was wrong. My stepdaughter-to-be helps heal that wound. She shows me that I'm not damaged or broken, because of who wasn't in my life. She still hugs me the same. All I need to do is try my best. And I'm thankful that my best is enough for her.

I have my fiancé. Amir helps me understand my value when I feel unworthy. He helps me understand my beauty when I feel ugly. He helps me find my confidence when I don't have any. And he continues to help me grow on my journey to self-love. Our relationship isn't perfect, but it's genuine. We teach each other how to love. Life definitely wouldn't be as interesting without him.

And lastly, I have me. I'm a survivor of many things. I've definitely been surrounded by Angel's my entire life. I've experienced a lot of traumatizing situations. Anyone of them could have broken me.

I remember being trapped in the bathroom with the gunman at Pulse. I was the most scared I had ever been in my entire life. I remember begging God to take my soul out of my body. I remember begging God to end my life. I'm so glad that he didn't. I choose to live. And living, truly living is a lot harder than surviving.

Lesson #11: All pain has a purpose.

The pain you went through is not in vain,
  The hail, the sleet, the snow, the rain,
  Different types of storms have clouded your days,
  You Cried, You fought, You Lost, You Prayed

No answer seemed to come your way,
  You gave up, You fell, You turned away,
  Too many demons to battle, to conquer, to slay
  Too tired, too wounded, too hurt to say

The horrible things that haunt you inside,
  Despite those things you continue to RISE
  You don't just SURVIVE,
  You LIVE, You WIN, You SOAR,
  Like a lion in the jungle,
  You EAT, You ROAR.